REFLECTIONS ON

Ineffable Love

Books by Cheryl Lafferty Eckl

Personal Growth & Transformation

A Beautiful Death:
Keeping the Promise of Love

A Beautiful Grief:
Reflections on Letting Go

The LIGHT Process:
Living on the Razor's Edge of Change

Wise Inner Counselor Books
Reflections on Being Your True Self in Any Situation
Reflections on Doing Your Great Work in Any Occupation
Reflections on Ineffable Love: from loss through grief to joy

Poetry for Inspiration & Beauty

Poetics of Soul & Fire

Bridge to the Otherworld

Idylls from the Garden of Spiritual Delights & Healing

Sparks of Celtic Mystery:
soul poems from Éire

A Beautiful Joy: Reunion with the Beloved
Through Transfiguring Love

Twin Flames Romance Novels

The Weaving:
A Novel of Twin Flames Through Time

Twin Flames of Éire Trilogy
The Ancients and The Call
The Water and The Flame
The Mystics and The Mystery

A Wise Inner Counselor Book

REFLECTIONS ON

Ineffable Love

from loss through grief to joy

Cheryl Lafferty Eckl

FLYING CRANE PRESS

REFLECTIONS ON INEFFABLE LOVE:
FROM LOSS THROUGH GRIEF TO JOY
© 2022 Cheryl J. Eckl, LLC
A Wise Inner Counselor™ Book
Wise Inner Counselor™

All poems and epigraphs © 2015 - 2022.
Excerpts from *A Beautiful Death: Keeping the Promise of Love* © 2010 -2022

Published by Flying Crane Press, Livingston, Montana 59047
Cheryl@CherylEckl.com | www.CherylEckl.com

Library of Congress Control Number: 2021921636
ISBN: 978-1-7346450-9-5 (paperback)
ISBN: 978-1-7367123-4-4 (e-book)

The information and insights in this book are solely the opinion of the author and should not be considered as a form of therapy, advice, direction, diagnosis and/or treatment of any kind. This information is not a substitute for medical, psychological or other professional advice, counseling or care. All matters pertaining to your individual health should be supervised by a physician or appropriate healthcare practitioner. Neither the author nor the publisher assumes any responsibility or liability whatsoever on behalf of any purchaser or reader.

Cover art by David W. Moore

Printed in the United States of America

For Stephen

As death is a gateway to realms of light
for those who must leave this world,
so is grief a portal to the soul
for those who remain.

Though the journey be different,
the destination is the same:
Joy!

*In times of sublime connection
with joy's indescribable "something,"
it seems to lend us
a surge of courage—
an exhilarating realization
that we are made of joyful stuff.*

CONTENTS

Author's Note

Y ou hold in your hands a book of hopes and dreams, of visions and ecstasies, of peaks and valleys, of trials and triumphs and of the connection between two hearts—one in this world and one in the next.

Contained in these pages are scenes from a life that, of necessity, contains loss. And with loss comes separation. Such is the nature of existence here on earth.

Yet, if we keep our hearts open and follow the inner guidance that speaks to us as the voice of Love, one day our lives may be flooded with a radiant joy that bridges worlds in wondrous moments of unity.

Love Is Stronger Than Death

While I have walked the rough road of loss and grief from the passing of my beloved husband and twin flame, Stephen, many experiences have proved to me again and again that love is not only stronger than death, love transcends death.

In the midst of the worst thing ever to occur in my life, I made an amazing discovery. Although Stephen was no longer alive on earth—enfolded in the profound love we still shared, our souls were able to communicate through the veil separating this world and the next.

A Way of Life

As we have pursued the concerted spiritual effort required to sustain that sublime connection, the unity of our twin flames has become a way of life. The presence of Stephen's spirit has replaced his physical absence with blessings of love, practical guidance and the warmth of his smile that cheered the hearts of all who met him.

Through a deep examination of how our souls have been renewed and how we each continue to evolve, writing this book has opened a portal of dramatic self-discovery that I never expected.

I should not have been surprised.

For, truly, have I come to know that loss is for our learning, grief is for our transformation and the joy that birthed us in the beginning is waiting to welcome us Home to realms of light.

The Time Has Come

This is the path of ineffable love I am blessed to walk with my beloved's presence alive in my heart.

Now the time has come to tell you the story of what I have learned so far—beginning with a poem that astonished me when it appeared eleven years after Stephen's passing.

Cheryl Lafferty Eckl

WHEN GRIEF DEPARTS

I am no longer your companion,
declared Grief one day—
an astonishing surprise to one
who had surrendered to heartache's
continuous company.

I have taught you all I can, said Grief,
about perseverance
and your determination
to face me squarely,
look me in the eye and forge a new life
through waves of disappointment
and unavoidable sadness.

When those who mourn
learn my secrets, I must depart.

And thus you have done—
plumbing my depths,
pushing back up from the bottom,
catching your breath,
then diving in again
to explore the dim waters
and dark caverns I hide from all
but the most intrepid swimmers.

Few know me as a Light force,
though I am the Divine's answer to loss
given before you dare to ask,
tucked away in your heart of hearts
against the day when Love
would break you open
(as it inevitably will)
and send you running
to the very core of all that is holy
in your True Self.

Oceanic am I,
and some think me cruel
in my stirring of
the body of sorrow.

Still, you found me out
and learned to surf my waves,
transmuting darkness into Light
in fires of creativity.

What am I, if not a flame—
agent of refiner's fire,
partner of my incandescent sister Joy,
who leaps out from your fractured heart
with golden gifts of pure insight,
forgiveness, gratitude and faith
that Love is ever stronger than death.

I, Grief, bid you *adieu*;
my work is finished,
at least for now.

Should I appear at some later hour,
please welcome me as an honored guest,
for you will know what I am about,
and I will trust you to fulfill
the spiral of our partnership.

And, lest you fear to entertain me again,
Joy has promised to remind you
of her previous gifts
while she waits her turn
to brighten the day.

Few understand that we serve together,
though we always have and always will.[1]

PART ONE

Wondrous
Moments of Unity

We do not find joy.
It arrives simply,
suddenly—as if delivered
by an unseen hand.

Joy finds us
and changes us forever.

Chapter One

My Soul's Destination

From the time I was a child, glimpses of heavenly realms have appeared and stayed with me as vivid reminders that Spirit is as close as a heartbeat. The most stunning vision of all came one day after my beloved husband passed from this life.

Enfolded in Joy and Oneness

On the morning after Stephen's soul took flight to other worlds, I awoke with sunlight streaming through the skylights in my bedroom and the words "There is joy in heaven!" ringing in my ears.

At first, I thought I was hearing angels announcing my sweetheart's victorious arrival in realms of light. Then I realized I was hearing Stephen's voice declaring his discovery that joy pervades the Other Side of life. He was in total ecstasy, and he was sharing it with me.

I was with him—we two—united in the bliss of a sublime dimension of being. My entire body was tingling with energy. I was bathed in a sphere of light, surrounded in an orb of pure radiance. For hours I was cradled in the tangible comfort and joy Stephen was beaming to me.

He was letting me know he was safe by wrapping me in the oneness of ineffable love. Within that luminous sphere, I could feel him pulling me to his heart while pouring out waves of gratitude for my seeing him through his passing.

Endings and Beginnings

Eventually, the glory faded and I found myself alone in our bedroom, feeling desperately sad. Although basking in communion with my beloved remained an inspiring memory, I did not yet know that our shared experience was also my soul's destination.

Only later did I realize that we were aiming for the same starry realms of illumination and joy. Those hours we shared enfolded in oneness were the fulfillment of vows we had made, even before this life. I promised Stephen that I would walk up to the door of death with him, and he promised me that his heart would be mine forever.

Our shared joy was also the initiation of a mystical journey that would lead us beyond physical separation to soul unity. In time, we would discover profound depths of connection through our love that grows stronger every day.

Before that communion would come to fruition, however, I had miles to travel on my own through some very dark days.

When Loss Broke Me Open

Even when touched by the light of heavenly realms, no life can be only smooth sailing. I know all too keenly the rough waters of loss. Despite those wondrous hours enfolded in joyful ecstasy, Stephen's death plunged me to the bottom of what seemed like a deep, dark well. I felt stripped of all I had held most dear, and my heart did not fully heal for many years.

When loss broke me open, grief rushed in to fill the abyss with a physical and emotional power that seemed as if it would destroy me. In fact, it had come to set me free, but that realization did not dawn until I had allowed grief to forge the next phase of my soul's path to wholeness.

Grief's Departure

As I pursued healing throughout the next decade, I shared what I was learning about the grief journey. I wrote several books, countless blogs and a lot of poetry. I conducted workshops and retreats, and I talked to hundreds of people who were walking their own rough road through loss and bereavement.

Late one evening, I entered into a sublime meditation with Stephen's spirit where a series of poems began to emerge. While I was writing verses about learning to dance on the bridge between this world and the next, *When Grief Departs* came bursting onto the page.

A Signal from the Universe

I was startled by the suddenness of the poem's appearance, though not its content. Sparks of joy had been kindling in me for quite some time. This new poem's stunning declaration simply reinforced a transcendent process that had become so much a part of me that I had not taken notice of the change.

I embraced *When Grief Departs* as a signal from the Universe that I should acknowledge what had shifted in my world since Stephen's death. Although other bereaved persons had told me that you never get over grief—you just get through it—the stanzas of this poem were affirming that (even subconsciously) I need not accept the idea that sorrow lasts forever.

Grief Completes the Work of Loss

I am convinced that the ability to grieve is an innate power, a quality of soul. Truly a divine gift—"given before you ask." If bereavement were any less powerful, it would not contain the energy necessary to complete the transformation which dramatic loss begins.

Grief compels us to dig deep into the core of our being. We must summon creative resources which may have been lying dormant in us for years. In the process, we learn to trust our inner guidance. We gain faith in its vibrant wisdom that beckons us into the sanctuary of the heart where separation does not exist.

Building Bridges of Light and Love

Since those moments of wondrous unity following Stephen's passing, I have never been the same. Nor would I want to be. The memory of those sensations lives in my heart as an image and a calling that inspires me and gives me hope for myself and for all who have been visited with loss.

I know first-hand—Once touched by the radiance which exists beyond the boundaries of time and space, we have an opportunity to live with a foot in two worlds.

This reciprocal, creative communication between realms can be a source of inspiration at all levels of existence. Daily, I am motivated to continue building bridges of light and love between my earthly life and "the core of all that is holy."

Here in my heart of hearts is a dimension of being where my soul and Stephen's commune in the clarity and totality of love that once was fleeting and now is simply here, where I am.

As Stephen's abiding presence makes clear, the path of self-discovery never ends, even when we take flight from this world. Whether through death or grief, our soul's joyful arrival in realms of ineffable love is the goal.

Chapter Two

LISTENING TO THE VOICE OF LOVE

In the early days of writing this book, I wondered if anyone would believe my experience of grief's departure. Would I have the courage to claim such an event in a world beset with unthinkable losses and enormous grief?

Then one day a friend sent me some verses by Rumi, the thirteenth-century Persian poet and Sufi mystic known as the "Poet of Love." Although I have always been inspired by how his poems speak so poignantly to my soul, I was not familiar with these remarkably appropriate stanzas:

Joy lives concealed in grief.

I saw grief drinking a cup of sorrow and called out,
It tastes sweet, does it not?
You've caught me, grief answered,
and you've ruined my business.
How can I sell sorrow,
when you know it's a blessing?

I had to laugh at this serendipitous connection. Here was Rumi, reaching out from centuries in the past, encouraging me to tell my story in the present.

Still, I was not as surprised by what Rumi said as how he said it. In these lines I recognized the voice of the muse upon whom I rely for my own poetical expressions.

Rumi was using language that sounded as if grief were personified and acting like a dramatic character who was capable of conversing with the poet. My muse did the same in *When Grief Departs*.

Plato and others have referred to the milieu that invites the muse to speak as the province of poets, artists, musicians and inventors. To that list I would add spiritual seekers and mystics. In this state, the individual's soul taps into a wondrous realm that feels divinely inspired in the way it operates outside of the human thinking mind.

As I have meditated on how this phenomenon has appeared in my own life as a poet, storyteller and mystical writer, I have perceived my muse as an aspect of inner guidance.

A Poet and a Guide

For as long as I can remember, I have pursued listening to the still small voice of conscience as a spiritual practice.

Throughout the challenges of adolescence and early adulthood, I learned that my life went along with fewer mishaps and more blessings when I paid attention to the precise instruction of the inner guide.

I have come to know this personal presence as the voice of my True Self, or what I call my Wise Inner Counselor.[2] I experience its promptings, warnings and insights as coming from a best friend who perceives my human limitations and yet holds the vision of my spiritual potential. This friend unfailingly speaks for the capital "L" Love that flows from God.

After reading Rumi's stanzas, I realized that my Wise Inner

Counselor is also a divine poet as well as the source of practical guidance in every area of my life.

Reflecting on a Spiral of Partnership

When Grief Departs mentions a spiral of partnership. The term reminds me that grieving may invite us into a collaborative relationship as we move through our bereavement. When the poem first appeared, it set me to wondering how such an interaction might relate to my ongoing communion with Stephen.

When we become partners with someone, we enter into a relationship of mutual trust. We are meant to be "part" of each other. We bear a common burden and we do so out of love. We bond with our partner in a vow—silent or spoken—that we will see our cause through to a potentially joyous end.

Such is the commitment Stephen and I made to each other long ago. We have always seen ourselves as partners.

So, what about the spiral?

This is where we truly embark on a mystical journey. When I close my eyes, an image comes to mind of our twin souls reaching for the heavens on intertwining ribbons of light that look like a double helix—weaving around and around in ever-ascending spirals of refined consciousness and experience.

A Vivid Example

Not long after Stephen's passing, I discovered an actual, physical spiral at the Solomon R. Guggenheim Museum in New York City. Designed by Frank Lloyd Wright, the main gallery is an enormous nautilus-like structure that climbs up seven stories from the ground floor to a huge skylight of frosted glass that reminded me of a zodiac.

When I visited the gallery during the fiftieth anniversary

of the museum's opening, images of the design and construction process were the featured exhibit.

Although visitors were encouraged to take an elevator to the top and then walk down, I chose the opposite direction. Strolling from the bottom of the gallery all the way up to the top, I felt a heightened, physical energy being focused through the spiral's perfect geometry.

Museum as Metaphor

Looking through the lens of a spiritual partnership, I have an even greater appreciation for the architect's accomplishment. The Guggenheim is an apt metaphor for an eternally spiraling path of self-discovery which we are meant to walk with the voice of Love as our wise inner guide.

That path does not leave us as it found us. The spiral climbs. Turn upon turn, it transcends the past, even as it builds upon what came before. The spiral is open to the center, so you can see across. Yet, further insights are not revealed until you turn the next bend. That is exactly how the Frank Lloyd Wright exhibit unfolded on the museum walls.

I found that the effort required to climb the ramp, though gentle, encouraged thoughtful examination of each item before venturing on and up. Here was art within art, as the spiral informed how the visitor viewed each display in the context of the whole.

Listening as Never Before

Navigating the spiral as it manifests in grief is like traversing the Guggenheim's giant nautilus, although the walk with grief can be a lonelier one.

Unlike the crowds of museum visitors, our companion is

unseen. Yet, when we continue listening to that still small voice, our Wise Inner Counselor is with us every step of the way.

This does not mean the going will be smooth. It will not. However, inner guidance assures us that climbing the spiral of a divine partnership can lead to our transformation, even our enlightenment as to how we are growing in the process.

When we listen as we have never listened before, we can emerge from mourning as a wiser, more compassionate, truer Self than we were before loss turned our world upside down and we heard the inner guide speaking to us as the voice of Love.

During that day at the Guggenheim, I sensed an invitation from Stephen's spirit to explore the mystery of the spiral more deeply. I still do.

The Invitation

Won't you come with me?

Let us be pilgrims together
along the path that leads
from what we see
to where we only dare imagine.

Supernal realms await us
just beyond this sylvan glen,
and my heart longs
for us to share
a vision's celestial magic

where spirals of ethereal light
will take us deep
into illumined passages

glistening with morning dew
and fairy stars
a-twinkle overhead.

Mystic sojourners are we,
brought together
for a purpose
as heart to heart and hand in hand
we go exploring
across the bridge
that Love has built out of itself

to teach travelers like us
that other worlds
are joined by a numinous power

that none can wrest
away from hearts
attached as twins
forever loyal
in mutual devotion.

Please, take my hand,
let us embark.

Love's mystery is calling.[3]

Chapter Three

A PILGRIMAGE OF HOPE

We may become depressed by the overwhelming impact of loss and the fear that grief might last forever. Fortunately, our True Self is not similarly burdened.

In the midst of our mourning, the Wise Inner Counselor knows we are made of stronger stuff than we may perceive. This loving presence is the internal champion that urges us forward. It encourages us to have hope that the love we are made of has always been stronger than death.

To strengthen that hope, wise inner guidance may prompt us to embark upon a pilgrimage—a journey on the path of self-discovery which can carry us into states of refined awareness and stages of spiritual and psychological development.

Pilgrimage may also prove just how strong we are.

A Different Type of Travel

Before my life as a pilgrim began, I had traveled frequently. To England and France as a student. Back to England as a management course instructor. To many cities around the United States to live and perform as a singer and actress.

As a child, I had accompanied my parents on vacation. During those family road trips the focus was on visiting relatives, national parks and places where my parents had lived during the second World War.

We enjoyed historical sights and usually went to church,

but that was the extent of our spiritual focus. We were tourists, not pilgrims.

Learning the Way of the Pilgrim

To be a pilgrim is to choose collaboration between soul and Spirit for a voyage of holy purpose. We may only vaguely comprehend the reasons why we feel compelled to leave life's familiar environs to embark on a journey that launches us into the Unknown.

Yet go, we must.

Although we set sail for an external physical destination, the real reason for this voyage is interior and ethereal. We are seekers after divine connection. We desire illumination, soul restoration—perhaps even a spiritual awakening.

This upward trek demands that we dig deep. Day after day, we must summon inner strength of body, mind, heart, soul and spirit. We learn mindful attentiveness and we listen for divine guidance.

The pilgrim's path is full of surprises, and every turn in the road or swell of the sea offers new lessons and fresh insights. Often those insights open windows into how we resist the promptings that would willingly light the way over, under, around and through our self-created obstacles to higher consciousness.

So we keep moving, watching, listening. Attending to the otherworldly communion between the temporary and the eternal which has beckoned our pilgrim hearts since time began.

Approaching Grief as a Calling

Venturing into the uncharted territories of grief's domain is not usually a journey we would choose. It chooses us. Perhaps so we will learn the difference between tourism and pilgrimage.

Remaining a tourist in the land of loss will not heal the

great caverns of loneliness that threaten to swallow us. Staying on the surface of bereavement robs us of the transcendent connections that await us when we remember the Wise Inner Counselor's promise of illumination.

If grief represents a calling, then how shall we approach it? Certainly not as an enemy to be defeated, although considering it as a welcome guest (the poem's idea) may seem too big a stretch.

It was for me. However, when I waded into grief's untested waters with the reverence I learned as a pilgrim, I eventually did experience surprising moments of profound transformation.

Bridging Two Worlds

Pilgrimage has taken me to Ireland where I have learned a lot about grief. The akashic records[4] of the land's tragic history of loss and death and mourning are very tangible throughout the island. So are the energies of mysticism and prayerful devotion that go back millennia.

Every time I visit the Emerald Isle, I am reminded of the proximity of etheric realms I felt during Stephen's final days on earth. The ease of accessing dimensions of the Unseen I have found in the Irish landscape is similar to those poignant hours when—with one foot in this world and one in the next—my darling and I moved toward his passing.

That sort of ethereal dual citizenship is the way of the pilgrim. It can be the same for an awakened griever. Regardless of how we are called, our goal is sustained contact with realms of light. We seek sacred touchstones which may spark interior connections to elevate our souls and heal our hearts.

A Life of Perpetual Pilgrimage

During my first visit to Ireland, I made some significant and enduring discoveries about the ways of grief. Since then, you might say that my life has become one of perpetual pilgrimage. And you would be right.

I rejoice in the knowledge that my mystical adventure will continue—*in* and yet not entirely *of* this world. I awake each morning with a clearer understanding of my life's purpose, garnered from many lessons learned in walking the pilgrim's path with the spirit of my beloved Stephen in my heart.

With each sunrise, inner guidance gives me hope that more moments of wondrous unity are waiting for both of us. I can feel them hovering, just around the next turn on grief's spiral of sacred partnership where love transcends death.

PART TWO

Transcending Death

Once touched by joy,
we are never satisfied with less.

Joy is of the Divine,
a quality of the Self,
a reminder of our origin
in Love.

Chapter Four

DO SOULS RECONNECT AFTER DEATH?

Do you ever wish you could listen to a replay of the conversations that were conducted in heavenly realms before you were born into this life?

Imagine being reminded of the instruction you received and the vows you made when the challenges of living in a physical body seemed far away. You were probably thinking about meeting cherished friends and soul mates from the past. You might have been discussing the possibility that you and your soul's twin could be together in this life to complete your original mission.

If that were to transpire, what would be required of you to finish the work you were born for? Would you both live to advanced age? Or would one of you leave this life years before the other? Perhaps your mission would be better served by one of you remaining on earth and the other offering guidance and support from the invisible world.

If that were true, would you be able to connect after death? Was that even a possibility? Was such a connection divinely ordained? And if so, how would you do it?

Keeping Our Promise

I can easily picture Stephen and me being involved in discussions like this. When he was originally diagnosed with cancer, somehow I was not entirely surprised. I think I knew at a soul level that we had promised to face this challenge.

At the time, neither of us imagined that the diagnosis would eventuate in his death, let alone in our spiritual reconnection beyond the grave. Yet, when I consider the precise timing of our meeting and marrying, losing each other for a time and now working in tandem on opposite sides of an ethereal bridge, I can only conclude that these events had been planned. Perhaps not for lifetimes, but certainly before this one.

A Fleeting Moment of Farewell

Experiences like ours convince me that souls do reconnect after death, although the method, duration, frequency and purpose of those connections will be uniquely tailored to each individual.

Sometimes the soul's only purpose is to say good-bye.

Several years ago, a woman I had sung with on occasion was killed in a car accident. As it happened, I was gathered with some others who knew her when we learned the awful news.

There were several in the group who were better acquainted with our mutual friend than I, so I was surprised when I heard her saying, "You were always kind to me." Yet there she was, in a fleeting moment of farewell.[5]

Heartwarming Stories

I think departing souls really do want to let their survivors know they are safe and enfolded in the light and love that can characterize the world beyond this one.

Occasionally, people will ask if I am still in contact with Stephen's spirit. When I affirm that I am, they appear grateful that my experiences validate their own.

I have been told some heartwarming stories about loved ones or friends who stay in touch from heavenly realms. When I contemplate these connections, what comes to me is a sense of immense gratitude shared between souls. Those on earth are grateful for the tender care they are receiving from the Beyond and those in spirit are grateful to be recognized and received.

What Is Best for Soul Growth?

Some souls do reconnect after death for longer periods of time—particularly if they are called to service which can only be accomplished with a partner on either side of the veil between worlds.[6]

The content and duration of the connection seems to depend on whether sustaining that contact by working together (perhaps as they did in life) is the best way for each individual to advance their soul growth.

For Stephen and me, it appears that our ongoing collaboration is precisely what our souls require.

Chapter Five

SOUL MATES & SOUL FRIENDS

The term "soul mate" is a familiar one these days and is often used in reference to an almost universal desire to find the single great love of one's life. The reality is much richer than that.

During the course of our lives, we may share a soul-mate relationship with several individuals with whom we enjoy a strong, positive affinity through similar values, interests, goals and beliefs.

I have been blessed with a few extraordinary friendships that I count as soul mates. Although the context and duration of our acquaintance has varied, the common characteristic is a feeling of closeness, as if we were members of a soul family.

We share a deep, fraternal love and trust that transcends time and space. We may not see each other for years. Yet whenever we reconnect, the experience is as if no time has passed.

I have found that many people we meet on our path of self-discovery can be a friend or teacher. The timeless, spiritual heart-tie is what makes them soul mates.

A Parental Soul Mate

Sometimes a soul mate does exist in our actual family. Growing up, I would not have considered my father and me as soul mates. After all, he was my parent. He was a quiet man who treated everyone with respect—including his little daughter. He seemed to trust me, and we had a lot of fun during my childhood. Of course, that is not reason enough to claim him as a soul mate.

The difference is the sacred connection I felt when I meditated on our relationship. I saw clearly that my father had been caring for my soul, not merely having a good time playing games, teaching me to fish or helping me with homework.

Even after I left home and went to college, he remained my soul's protector. He was always the one to come to my rescue. When he died, I was devastated. At the time I did not understand why I was so heartbroken. Now I see that our bond would always have been soul deep, even if he had not been my father.

Past-Life Obligations

We may not be able to identify who is or is not a soul mate except in hindsight. For example, I do not consider my first husband as a soul mate. Although when I first met him, I felt a strong spark of recognition between us, our short-lived marriage was fraught with struggle and misunderstanding.

I came to realize that we had a karmic, past-life obligation which required our being married for a while. That was all.

The Soul Friend

Anam cara is an Irish term that means soul friend. I love this concept for its implication of loyalty and care between two people. They may have lived very different lives. And yet, when their paths cross, they instantly know each other.

They may strike up a conversation that seems to have begun in a past life and that can carry on unabated in this one. When one of my dear friends lost her *anam cara* to cancer only a couple of years after they had reconnected in this life, I wrote *Prayer for a Soul Friend* to comfort her.

During a recent pilgrimage in Ireland, I was prompted to

read the poem to my fellow travelers at our final dinner together. As it happened, two of the group had lost their spouses and were in the process of stepping into new romantic relationships back home. They were deeply moved and declared that I had surely written these verses for them.

Prayer for a Soul Friend

Anam Cara—that's how the Celts called
    the friend who will see you naked,
    unblemished by the world
    or your own misconceptions.

We humans suffer from mistaken identity.
    Assuming ourselves to be other than
    a brilliant soul created by Love,
    we act as unworthily as we
    believe ourselves to be.

Soul friends know otherwise—
    and slip into our lives
    to push, prod, humor and cajole us
    to look into their eyes and see
    the image of our loveliness
    mirrored back in purity's reflection.

This is gnosis—unschooled knowing—
    recognition deep and sudden
    that, at its core, bears no conditions,
    urging only courage, kindness and
    attunement with each soul's pledge
    to higher purpose.

All we really have in this life is time;
    and no one has tapped clear prophecy
    to give us the measure of that interval.

Such is the way of *anam cara* that
    cycles may be fleeting and
    lessons more than we can bear—
    or so we think.

But soul friends know that time
    is naught when put to use
    in loving our togetherness and
    cherishing the ties that bind us
    heart to heart—no matter what.

Our beloveds may lift off this plane,
    leaving us to mourn their flight;
    but gentle ears detect a whisper,
    reassuring those who grieve
    that lovers once may be lovers again.

For Love awakened cannot help but find itself
    renewed and recreated
    in life's sweet gift of a new companion
    who comes to share the path we choose
    to journey Home together.

Who would not pray for such a partner—
    if even for a little while?[7]

Chapter Six

THE MYSTERY OF TWIN FLAMES

While soul-mate relationships can dramatically enhance the lives of both partners, the urgent longing for our ultimate mate who will complete us as no other is based on a more intimate and ancient connection—that of the twin soul or twin flame.

Esoteric traditions, including Plato's writings, suggest that eons ago, in the beginning of our soul's evolution, we were created as a single, androgynous sphere of pure light energy which then divided into the polarities of yang and yin.

Throughout time, these two halves of a single whole retain the same foundational soul blueprint. At the very root of being, our gifts, mission and original divine plan are the same as our soul's twin. Only the two of us contain that exact pattern.

In this age, a challenge to many twin flames is that, over countless lifetimes, our souls have gone separate ways. We had meant to stay together forever. Instead, we made karma in the matter universe and developed characteristics that are quite unlike each other. Should we meet our twin flame in this life, we may not share equal affinity as we do with soul mates who are more like us in personality and preferences.

The idea that in this life we are destined to connect romantically with our soul's twin is often not the case. Even if twin flames do recognize each other, they may not be the same age or otherwise available for such a relationship.

The point of seeking our twin flame is to bring wholeness to the connection in whatever manner it appears. If we do not happen to meet that person physically, our love and devotion toward people we *do* know accrues to our other half. For good or for ill, our actions resonate with our twin flame—wherever that one may be, in heaven or on earth.

Acting "As If"

The unification of twin flames is a complex spiritual equation which can be quite incomprehensible to our outer minds. The fact that some twin flames are markedly different from each other or have significant negative karma between them means that an inner refinement of consciousness must take place before the Divine will attempt bringing them together.

That is one reason why we do not grasp after our twin flame. Trying to decide if we and our current partner are each other's twin can unintentionally burden the relationship. So, we act "as if" and let the voice of Love plot our course.

This is where soul mates are often stand-ins for the twin flame. In any case, we do our best to treat every relationship as if the other person were our twin.

A Natural Outcome

If we happen to recognize and marry our soul's twin, we may experience the most sacred of love trysts—a divine romance which takes place in our heart of hearts where the True Self is fully present in each of us.

This holy communion is not only *how* our twin flames continue to work together beyond the grave, it is also *why* we do. The process is a natural outcome of mutuality. If we are individually becoming congruent with our original soul blueprint, it stands to reason that we would be moving into congruency with each other—even if we are physically light-years apart.

Some twin flames will achieve reunion while they are both alive. For others, like Stephen and me, the road to soul unity can be a challenging one. Although we shared a profound love in the knowledge of our being twin flames, we did not find our way to oneness until our earthly life together was coming to a close.

A Calling to Connect

As Stephen neared the end of his life, the intensity of our love increased as we became all too aware that we were about to lose each other. Then one day, an even greater bonding took place. If we had ever doubted that we were twin flames, this event sealed us in the knowledge of who we would always be to each other.

While reading to Stephen from *The Little Prince* by Antoine de Saint-Exupéry, I came to a passage in which the Fox is explaining to the Little Prince how we tame who or what we are responsible for. I realized that Stephen and I were like that. We had tamed each other in this life. He had calmed me down and I had opened him up.

Immediately, the image of a waist-high stone wall (like you find in Ireland) appeared in my mind's eye. Here was a metaphor for the obstacles that had separated us.

In that moment, the wall simply slid down into the ground, leaving us standing in an open field on either side of what had been a barrier, now beholding each other totally and completely as two halves of the same whole.

A Spiritual Acceleration

I would not be who I am today without Stephen's death. I know we would not be able to pursue the mission we were born to complete unless one of us had taken up residence on the Other Side of an ethereal bridge between worlds.

As I write this, I am struck with a possibility that the one to depart this life could have been me in the single-car accident I survived during the summer of our seventh year of marriage.

I wonder—Did we have a choice about who would stay and who would go? Was there a question about when or how that separation might transpire?

My sense is that our souls knew we needed more time to deepen our bond, to overcome more of our mutual karma and to gain the individual spiritual and psychological wholeness that could sustain the thread of contact we would need once Stephen passed on.

His having cancer over a period of four-and-a-half years brought us together in a way that no other experience could have done. In fact, in his last week of life, he said to me, "Don't you think this cancer has been a spiritual acceleration for both of us?"

I had to agree. And now I see a greater wisdom in the path we have been called to walk.

Chapter Seven

ANSWERING THE CALL OF LOVE

When death takes from you the love of your life, you must become the love of your life. That is one of the greatest lessons I have learned since Stephen left this world.

I recently read a story about a couple who had been married for seventy-five years. The husband declared that he was even more in love with his wife today than when he married her.

That is my experience with Stephen. As my love for him has grown, my desire to become the fullness of my True Self has intensified. Today I feel a greater impetus to achieve our ultimate reunion with each other and with the Divine than I did when we were married.

In the early days after Stephen's passing, I was more keenly aware of missing him—desperately.

A Serious Quandary

Stephen did not expect us to be in contact once he died. In fact, he told me not to try to find him on the Other Side. Although he believed we would always be a part of each other in spirit, somehow he saw himself sailing off to other worlds where we would not be in touch.

The fact that he was able to immediately share his new-found joy with me must have come as a surprise to him. It did to me. I had never considered that my soul could be transported into spontaneous unity with him.

Sadly, despite that wondrous experience, I was not able to retain a feeling of oneness. Instead, I struggled between remembering Stephen's instruction not to try to locate him after he was gone, while at the same time strongly feeling his presence.

One of the important lessons I had learned in our marriage was to take him at his word. He thought very carefully about situations, and his conclusions were usually correct. So I was in a serious quandary about what to believe—his parting words or my own intuition.

The Bonding

The summer after Stephen's passing, I decided to go on a pilgrimage to Ireland with a small group of spiritual seekers. Uppermost in my mind was a powerful intuition that I could reconnect with my beloved's spirit in the thin places of the Emerald Isle.

Unfortunately, I was trying to *make* the connection happen, which, of course, it didn't. Not until the next-to-last day of exploring Celtic holy sites did I finally stop trying.

Our group had arranged to meet Sister Mary Minehan at the visitor center of the Brigidine Sisters in Kildare.[8] For two inspiring hours, she shared with us her understanding of what it means to be a pilgrim and how the Celtic mind interprets the cycles of birth, growth, harvest and death as one continuous flow. Her discourse penetrated to the very depths of my soul.

At the end of her talk, the other people in the group returned to the tiny sedan that was our transportation around the lush Irish countryside. I stayed behind. When Sister Mary and I were alone, I told her how much her words had meant to me because I had recently lost my husband to cancer.

"Then your heart is fractured, isn't it," she said with great compassion.

"Yes," I wept, "And I don't think I can bear it."

"Well, you know he's right here," Sister Mary stated as a matter of fact. She focused her clear blue eyes on mine and said firmly, "You're strong. You can do this and you must."

I gulped back my tears, took a deep breath and managed to say, "I will."

I'll never know if Sister Mary actually saw Stephen's spirit or if her firm belief that our deceased loved ones are never far from us was her reasoning. Regardless, she gave me a hug as if she would infuse me with a strength that flowed from her own profound spiritual connection.

In that moment of her affirmation of my beloved's presence and my willingness to persevere, I experienced my soul and Stephen's spark together in a bonding we have never lost.

As I made my way back to the car to rejoin my fellow pilgrims, I knew I had received a healing that was more complete than I could have hoped for and exactly what I needed in a way I never could have made happen on my own.

Other Souls Like Ours

When I discovered Cynthia Bourgeault's inspiring memoir, *Love Is Stronger than Death: The Mystical Union of Two Souls*,[9] I knew I had found a kindred spirit. Reading her book was an electrifying example of the type of ongoing mission which Stephen and I share—with one soul in this world and one in the next.

Cynthia recalls the two completely unexpected years she spent with Brother Rafe, a fellow hermit-monk who turned out to be the love of her life.

Rafe was twenty years Cynthia's senior and appeared to be in reasonably good health. However, they believed his time on earth was short, so they worked with great intensity to overcome any obstacles that would prevent them from communicating after his passing—which was his intention.

They felt called to forge a mystical path of love in a soul connection that would continue from "here to eternity." In fact, almost immediately after Rafe's passing, he began supporting and guiding Cynthia from beyond the veil.

Overcoming Resistance

Cynthia writes about having to overcome her resistance to aligning her consciousness with Rafe's inner life, which meant she was resisting her own inner life. Once she had assimilated the unconventional approach to their spiritual and personal relationship that he had been trying to impart to her, she admitted to becoming more like Rafe—and more like her True Self.

I encountered a similar challenge with Stephen. My subduing an outer, synthetic self that was resistant to the wisdom path he wanted me to walk with him was necessary for me to gain the rich inner life that my soul had always yearned for.

Allowing grief to strip me of that false identity was also necessary to seal the tie that enables our ongoing communication. As I have continued to internalize aspects of our mutual soul blueprint, I know I have become more like Stephen than I used to be.

A Journey Beyond Imagining

Today, he and I are alive in each other. Answering love's call to this divine romance has been a journey unlike any we could have imagined.

Knowing that our mission and soul growth as twin flames is far from over, we work diligently to retain and strengthen the connection we are blessed to share.

Chapter Eight

RETAINING THE THREAD OF CONTACT

One of Stephen's favorite spiritual readings was about the process of making the transition from this world to the next. He was fascinated by life after death and eagerly strove to prepare himself for the journey.

He believed that immediately after death we retain the same level of enlightenment we had achieved in life. So, his intention in the months and weeks before his passing was to increase what he called his "spiritual gravity"[10] or "spiritual receptivity."

Once he crossed over, he wanted to be in sync with that luminous state. He saw himself sailing into a bright new world with enough attainment to hit the etheric ground running and immediately begin to learn how life works on the Other Side.

A Period of Adjustment

What Stephen was sensing was a necessary period of adjustment for the newly departed. If many spiritual teachings are correct that only the physical body is left behind in death, I could easily understand the adventure he anticipated in learning to function with a new light body.

In his final days, as the combination of disease and pain medications weakened his ability to think clearly, he would often declare, "I can't wait to have a brain that works."

He was definitely looking forward to an existence without the limitations of a compromised mind and body.

Since his passing, Stephen and I have done a lot of adjusting. I frequently have had to shift my perspective about myself and our relationship. And I sense that he continues to go through his own changes.

A Cosmic Buddy System

Occasionally, I receive e-mails from men and women who have also lost the love of their life. One strong theme in their correspondence is the desire to stay in contact with their departed beloveds. Several of them have commented that their partners led them to my work.

I am always touched by the thought that souls abiding in the etheric know what I am doing here on earth. Then I remember that Stephen is on the Other Side, spreading the word.

I believe he occasionally supports the recently departed in a kind of buddy system—helping them adjust to their new circumstances. My part, then, is to encourage those of us who remain here on earth to follow our Wise Inner Counselor when it comes to discerning if we are meant to commune with our departed loved ones.

We do not attempt to take heaven by storm. This sublime communion between souls is a contact we cannot force or control. Aligning our will with the Divine is the only power that can open the connection—and only for holy purpose.

Entering a State of Heightened Awareness

We do not cling to the past. On the contrary—Stephen and I use our shared history as a springboard to the new tomorrows that honor what went before.

We acknowledge the love that grows between us and we respect the spiritual requirements for each of us to accelerate on the path of liberating our souls from karmic cycles of rebirth. We do our best to enter into a state of heightened awareness that is open to collaboration yet does not clamor after it.

Although I feel Stephen with me almost constantly these days, there have been phases in our relationship when I knew he was off in other parts of the galaxy. Fortunately, he seems to have an ability to go about his business on the Other Side while never losing sight of me.

How Stephen and I Connect

A friend recently asked me what was most precious to us in our relationship. Was there, perhaps, a special item we had purchased together? I laughed when I realized that Stephen and I primarily bought furniture because neither of us had owned a house before. I still have those pieces and I cherish them, but home furnishings were not what we valued most.

What was most precious to us was our love of uplifting words and ideas that we discovered in philosophy, poetry and spiritual literature. On Sundays we would read together from our favorite authors and share the spontaneous insights that occurred as we were reading.

Stephen was particularly fond of Wordsworth's poetry, which he often read aloud to me. Looking back, I can see how those hours spent basking in the beauty of the spoken word were establishing our unique soul connection that would continue beyond the veil.

Nowadays, whenever I write (especially poetry), I feel Stephen very near. If he has an idea he wants me to understand quickly and clearly, I may hear him speak a few words. And those words often come with a brief impression of his face or form so I know the idea is from him.

At other times, his thoughts come to me as a tangible, felt sense that conveys a complete image or impression. I may simultaneously hear and feel these sparks imprint themselves in my being with a savor of his essence, which is unique from mine. I can tell the difference between my own thoughts and those of Stephen—particularly in the way they arrive.

From Here to Eternity

We share an ever-present heart tie. Our ability to connect is always available and the contact can be made in an instant. When I rest my attention on Stephen, I feel him nestled in my heart, which burns in the presence of his love.

Will our work continue into eternity?

I pray it will, although in what manner only God knows. The character of our ongoing mission will likely depend on how our collaboration develops in the next couple of years. As I know so well, the future must be lived to be known.

The concept of letting go is very strong for me these days, although the question remains—Letting go of what? I am not letting go of my mission with Stephen. Nor am I letting go of my life; that is not my call.

Rather, I am letting go into God, into the light of my heart, into the joy that my beloved does his best to remind me is the calling, the origin of our souls and the goal of our tomorrows.

All else remains a mystery and I am content with that.

Chapter Nine

CLEARING THE WAY TO JOY

When I am in focused attunement with my True Self, I notice that I am joyful. More than feeling emotionally happy or elated, I experience a grounded sense of peace, vitality and capability. This leads me to consider that joy is the nature of the True Self—that living my life in consonance with my Wise Inner Counselor leads to joy.

I do know that my inner guide's insistence that I move past merely coping with loss to creating a process of partnering with grief made all the difference in the early days following Stephen's passing. And that process did lead to joy.

Questions About Coping
While researching the meaning of "to cope," I was surprised to find it defined as "to resist."

What might I be resisting? I wondered. What aspect of my lesser self might be pushing away a divine gift of healing?

Going deeper into the question, I wondered if coping could be a type of accommodation with that lesser self—the part of us that clings to its familiar mindsets.

Is merely coping a refusal to give up our attachments—for example, to familiar spiritual beliefs? Would we rather keep our well-worn practices and escape into the rituals we know instead of entering into the transformed spirituality that grief offers?

Getting stuck in coping could be denying our ability to heal our grief. If we shun the bereavement process, are we refusing to be transformed? Do we prefer revolving the pain of our situation rather than resolving the challenges of loss?

Do we really desire self-pity? Do we want to remain sad, weepy—even angry—instead of discovering the profound peace our soul longs to experience? Or are we simply desperate for another solution to our grief that we have not discovered yet?

Our Greatest Ally

Rumi offers an approach that is different from resisting the mind-numbing pain of loss. In another quote he says that pain can become our greatest ally.

How can that be?

Perhaps one reason is that pain shines a light on our helplessness and sends us running to the heart of our Wise Inner Counselor. When our human mind fails to show us a way out of the agony of loss, inner guidance urges us to enter into the transformational alchemy that grief can effect in us. In the process, when we become humble and malleable as clay in the hand of a divine potter, grief may depart and joy may emerge.

Stephen did his best to accelerate that process in me when he beamed his joy into my being for just a little while. I wonder— Was this experience meant to show me the powerful light that can shine out from twin flames when they are finally united, so I would never forget?

That seems right. And I have caught a glimpse of that radiance at least once more since my sweetheart's departure.

A Joyful Reunion

Several years ago, I felt Stephen encouraging me to attend the memorial service for the elderly father of a dear friend. Their large Irish family was gathering at a charming old church where, only six weeks earlier, we had celebrated the life of the father's deceased wife.

That lovely woman had been the mother of my friend and his siblings and the cherished grandmother to a bevy of young adults from the next generation. She was also the twin flame of the much-loved man whose life we were honoring.

The family created a beautiful tribute to their father and grandfather. Now that he and his twin flame were together in realms of light, the poignant remembrances sparked a tangible presence of devotion between the couple that transcended time and space.

The memorial affected me deeply. Throughout the service I could feel Stephen reminding me that this is the sublime joy of twin flames united in spirit. He wanted me to witness how our souls may finally arrive at a realization that nothing less than love ever happened—because we will have become that love.

After the service, I sat in my car for quite some time as the words of the following poem flooded my being and did not leave me alone until I had recorded them.

A Beautiful Joy

A beautiful joy occurs
    when God is present,
    when worlds are joined
    across a bridge of unselfish love;
    holiness is its flavor
    and mercy its expression.

Tears come—
    not from sadness,
    though loss may be the impetus;
    but more from recognition
    that this is what Home feels like:

        the utter acceptance
        of one's being
        of one's gifts
        even of one's failings
        and of one's longing
        to be more of that—

            that openness
            that givingness
            that tenderness
            that fullness
            that indescribable
                something

        that knits up hearts
        in unity and care,
        making all unlike itself pale
        and fall away, as if nothing less
        than pure Love ever happened.[11]

Chapter Ten

FINDING A GREATER LOVE

I was not capable of fully loving Stephen when he was alive. Not the way I love him now. Now that I have learned to love myself. Now that I feel my heart opening and expanding in a way it never did before.

I have had to live my way into that kind of love by continually stripping away those elements of my lesser self that are selfish, mean, petty or fearful.

Loss will do that. Sometimes losing who you love more than life itself is the only way to discover the humility that nurtures selflessness and surrender—that brings you to your knees in the knowledge that you haven't a clue about how to treasure the life you have been given or to cherish yourself in the living.

Inner and Outer Congruency

Stephen knew a lot about treasuring life. He was a great friend to his inner world. He cherished the peace and harmony he found there and strove to bring those qualities to the outer world he inhabited with a great deal of grace.

I do not know if he would have acknowledged loving himself, although he was certainly comfortable in his own skin. He simply was who he was—a man of integrity. One sensed about him an integration of his inner and outer worlds. He was a man who walked his talk.

Of course, he had his struggles. Everyone does. Still, he

brought those struggles to prayer and meditation and communion with his God. I know he found profound answers in the sanctuary of his heart because of how he occasionally spoke about his spiritual path.

This is the person he shared with me in our marriage. There were many moments when I was able to receive that gift. Certainly, in the weeks before his departure from this world when the veil between the Unseen and the seen thinned to the faintest of curtains.

Since then, I have written my way into many points of understanding that have come to me over the years following Stephen's passing. In the process, I have more fully entered into communion with my own mystical spirit that I know to be who I am at heart.

An Accelerated Journey of Self-Discovery

The Universe needs twin flames to be permanently joined. Their reunion is one of the greatest powers in the Cosmos when that tie springs from equal love and spiritual attainment in both partners—when each twin becomes one with their inner divinity and brings that wholeness to the other.

Doing my part for the ultimate union of our twin flames is my focus now. The past thirteen years since Stephen left for other realms have been an accelerated journey of self-discovery.

I have learned to appreciate myself, to cherish and honor the divine spark that lives within me. I have forged a daily practice of listening to my Wise Inner Counselor in a way I did not do until that voice became my lifeboat through Stephen's illness and passing, and my lifeline to his heart.

The more I have come to know and love my own reality, the nearer Stephen's spirit has drawn—to the point that I now experience his presence more than his absence.

When tears come nowadays, the reason is proximity, not distance. In those moments, the intensity of Stephen's love is so strong that my soul rises to my heart and fills me with such holy passion that I weep in recognition of our oneness.

Stephen and I adore our individual soul divinity, even as we acknowledge each other's presence alive in our heart of hearts. That unity energizes our love and expands it in service to other twin flames, whom we long to help understand this remarkable calling.

In this light of Stephen's inspiration, my pilgrim path spirals ever upward—often in sublime moments when my love reaches straight through the veil between worlds to meet him where he is.

Contact

You will know we have connected
when tears come;
the tears that tell true,
dissolving separation
in an instant.

Doubt cannot enter here
and nothing bad ever happened
when you are at my side.

The fire of my affection burns
like a precious chest wound,
singing of Home and oceans of Love
whose waves lap the shore
of my soul, chanting:
We are one.
We are one.
We are one.

Come, sit with me a while
and learn a secret:

Eternity is a hologram,
a glistening, swirling blue bauble
held in the palm of Spirit's hand,
where contact goes on forever
in the flow of smiles and tears
and ineffable joy.[12]

Chapter Eleven

THE LEGACY OF OUR LOVE

Do any of us ever really know what our legacy will be? How we will be remembered—if at all? What contribution will we have made to life before our brief span on earth is over?

Sometimes a glimpse of that contribution comes in a vision of what we may recognize as our sacred labor.

Our Continuing Purpose

When we learned that Stephen's cancer was terminal, I had a vision that, once he passed on, he was to be my inspiration from the Other Side. I was to remain alive on earth and write a book to tell our story.

I had already been journaling about the events that had transpired since his original diagnosis two years earlier. After receiving such clear and inspiring direction, I made a point of writing down everything that happened as our lives unfolded over the next two-and-a-half years.

My memoir, *A Beautiful Death*,[13] was the result. At the time, I could not have guessed that we would be commissioned to continue recording our ongoing experiences with one of us on either side of the veil between worlds. Yet that remains our work.

Teachers at Heart

One way to identify a legacy is to delve into how we approach daily life. Another is to create a mission statement.

I developed this one for my self, and it definitely applies to both of us.

To learn, to love, to teach
so that others may have a better life.

We are teachers at heart. I followed in my father's foot-steps as a course author and instructor. Stephen was a natural teacher who created streamlined systems and then taught his co-workers how to use them to save time and effort. Before he got sick, he talked about becoming a tutor after he retired.

A Course in Miracles says that we each have students who can learn only from us essential lessons for their path forward in this life. Stephen and I take that statement seriously. We have vowed to continue sharing what we are learning for as long as God wills.

Mystics and Philosophers

I was born a mystic and became a philosopher when I married Stephen. He was born a philosopher and became a mystic as his spiritual path deepened into a profound meditation practice.

We interpret who and what we are (and how and what we have learned) in both physical and metaphysical terms. Together, ours is a path of lifelong learning—of seeking to understand the mysteries of the Universe and bringing them to earth.

We investigate the Unknown, learn some of its secrets and do our best to light the path for others. Our greatest desire is to demonstrate for twin flames the life that can be lived when you are willing to put in the spiritual and psychological effort to transmute the lesser self and bond with the True Self.

Then, and only then, do we entertain the possibility of com-munication after death as an ongoing connection that changes aspects, yet does not end.

This is our legacy and our experience as we have followed the guidance of our Wise Inner Counselor. Keeping our promise of love, we have come to the point of taking one hundred percent personal responsibility for ourselves while being one hundred percent dedicated to the victory of each other's soul.

Our Goal to Serve

It is the nature of Love to extend itself, to serve life, to raise up other people, to help them exceed the limitations of being human on planet Earth.

As our love grows, so does our desire to be of service. Life offers far more opportunities than time and space allow, which is the reality of my still living in a physical body. So, we focus on what makes us unique—our relationship as twin flames.

We understand better than many the intensity of that relationship. We continue to live its challenges and the potential for good that can be accomplished when twin flames enter into the sacred love tryst that can unite them for eternity.

Our goal is to offer insight into life's mysteries and to share with others the love that overflows our hearts when we are deeply attuned to each other. The presence of our love is the legacy we most desire to leave behind as inspiration for all who journey through life's many transitions.

PART THREE

Navigating Transitions

Joy is not of this world,
though it attends our important rites
of human passage—
a touch of heavenly celebration
when we transcend a difficult past
and wake up to a holy instant.

Chapter Twelve

RIDING WAVES OF TRANSITION

I once spent the better part of two days sitting by the Pacific Ocean, first near Carmel and then at Asilomar, California, allowing the immensity of sights and sounds to fill my soul with the eternal presence of the sea.

Yes, I thought, here is a metaphor for grief. Here there is a stillness, a gathering of energy before the next wave rolls in. Kissing the shore or crashing against giant rocky cliffs, each wave brings change—depositing sand or eroding the dunes, shaping and being shaped by the shore where it lands.

On the second day by the water, I slipped into a contemplative state of unity with the ocean's rhythms.

Breathing into the Thresholds - A Meditation

Like waves of the sea and waves of grief, each breath I take is a transition. Breath is constantly in motion. Energy gathers as I inhale.

I pause, ever so imperceptibly. Then I breathe out, blowing wind into my sails for the forward movement of life—knowing that one day will be my final exit into the next world.

Birth and death. Life's two great transitions. The first an inhalation, the last a final exhalation. I pause again and wonder—How does this metaphor help me ride the waves of transition? I pay attention to the energy within and around me. With every shift, I inhale. I am "in-spired." I notice the collection of life force and then I push out a breath and ride that wave all the way to the shore of its destination.

Waves breathe slowly in and out as each one spends its identity in a single journey to land.

I will take many breaths and ride many waves. The more awakened I am to how the waves of life and loss are breathing me in and out, the more fluidly I may navigate those changes that are taking me from here to there.

The pause at the top of a breath or a wave is a threshold where the energy changes from gathering in to flowing out. Here is a point of transition I recognize.

Still, if I am only peripherally aware of this razor's edge, I may not be prepared for its life-changing ride to shore. I must be attuned to the energy that is about to break before it does.

When a tsunami is dramatically pulling the ocean away from land, wild animals move to higher ground. They do not wait for the wave to come hurtling ashore in all its destructive power.

Can I do the same? During the apparent lull between life's transitions, when new thresholds are being formed moment by moment, how do I know to move to higher ground?

Inner guidance shows the way. I pay attention to being grounded in current circumstances. I seek higher, more refined levels of consciousness that offer clearer perspectives of challenges and opportunities.

I take care to patch the holes in my spiritual life

boat. I wax my imaginary surfboard. I make certain I am physically, mentally and emotionally strong. For I know that the next wave of transition is just over the horizon.

We Are Never in a Single Transition

We may be moving between jobs, states of health, stages of life or changes in relationships. The seasons clearly immerse us in those in-between times—when spring has not quite blossomed or the weather is still too warm to be winter. Nature is perpetually in flux. Plants and animals are constantly adapting to shifts in their environment.

I have spent months on the road—first as a singer in a band and later as a sales rep for a publishing company. I have changed jobs and careers and moved back and forth across the country more times than I can count. Whenever I found myself in a new situation, I wondered—How will this change unfold? What can I expect from it? What does it require of me? Does it contain untapped opportunities?

This movement between phases is where I discovered the creative potential within each new circumstance. Those transitions were frequently the most fertile soil for moments of self-discovery. They were also where I confronted fear—often in a new aspect of the great Unknown. Regardless of the course I believed I had set, the Unseen was the determiner of where I eventually landed.

Navigating the In-Between Times

Preschool teachers have told me that transitions are the most challenging segments of the school day. Children are frequently hesitant to leave their parents in the morning and then resist going home in the afternoon.

We are all a bit like that. Once we grow accustomed to one routine or pattern or rhythm, we are reluctant to break it. Transition throws us out of sync with what has become familiar, and we do not like it. We may gaze at the ocean for inspiration, but when the random waves of endings come upon us, we are faced with a choice of resisting as humans are wont to do or adjusting as Nature vividly demonstrates.

A Loss in Every Change

During the years when I worked for a large non-profit organization, many of my assignments involved being at the forefront of change—either planned by experts in reorganization or accidental as a result of people simply being people. Within those workplace experiences and my personal journey through life, I have learned that even welcome transitions can be disruptive.

Graduations, promotions, retirements, relocations, new relationships or babies may challenge our sense of self, which is one of the first casualties when we are asked to stretch out of the familiar. Every point of growth means leaving behind who we were in favor of stepping into the possibility of who we might become.

We may tell ourselves that a bit of loss does not warrant grief or tears. Especially not in comparison to the improvements that are being introduced or juxtaposed to the truly terrible losses that have visited us or others.

If that is so, then why do we feel nostalgic for the things we have chosen to replace? Perhaps it is because innovation requires more effort and greater courage.

Change is dark and mysterious in the way it unseats us from the familiar, making us strange to ourselves and opening up questions of purpose and place that we had not planned to ask.

We thought the murky Unknown emerged only with unwelcome change. But we enthusiastically planned this home renovation, retirement, new career, marriage or graduation. Or perhaps we courageously ended an unhealthy relationship. Or we moved on from a job that no longer supported our ability to advance or fully use our talents.

It was our idea to plot a new course. Yet suddenly, the familiar signposts are missing, and we find ourselves once more in the land of loss, accompanied by emotions that offer us a cup of sorrow along with the anticipated cup of cheer.

Another Mystery of Transition

The question is—Will we drink a small cup of sorrow that appears in the midst of even positive change? If we are attuned to life's in-breath and out-breath, we will say, "Yes."

Allowing ourselves to mourn the loss of those elements of external life or internal being that we are glad to release frees up the energy that was engaged in holding the old patterns together. We need that energy to nurture the new.

Here we discover another mystery of change—The old does not entirely pass away. While we transcend its outworn patterns, if we honor its liberation with our tears, its remaining positive qualities can become integrated into our wholeness.

Rites of Passage

Welcome change or necessary losses—they are all transitions, rites of passage. The novel builds upon the familiar, though only if we step aside for new shoots to push up through the fertile soil of our imagination.

No loss or disappointment or surprising turn of change is

too small or insignificant to be unworthy of our notice. We may weep. And as we do, the river of life moves on and our tears facilitate oneness with that flow.

Mourning proves how much we cared. It reminds us of the past's importance. And it lubricates the engine of change to create an invigorated future out of our love for what came before.

Facilitating Change

Have you ever found yourself precipitating change simply by being present? That has been my experience more than once. In fact, it has happened so often that I wrote a poem about having that effect on a variety of people and circumstances.

In a way, facilitating change has been the story of my life.

The Catalyst

She was a born change-maker.

Though she meant no harm,
situations and people made major shifts
when she came on the scene;

> and by the time she had moved on,
> no circumstance remained untouched,
>> not even the condition
>> of her own heart.

For life sent her into strange events
that puzzled her for many years,

> until she came to see the pattern
> of enthusiastic beginnings,
> her being filled with pluck and hope
> for what could be accomplished,
>> only to be met with anger,
>> stone walls and rejection
>> from those she'd come to help.

In early days, an innocence
had encouraged her to sally forth;

> but now when a deeper nature beckoned
> that she should seize a perilous cup,
>> her mind recalled in vivid scenes
>> the enigma of her lonely path,
>> in reluctant recollection
>> of the burden she would bear.

For even though she welcomed change
as life's essential principle,

most folks did not—and blamed her
for the consequence of their own deeds
    that her presence
    had simply brought to light.

She felt self-doubt impeding her path,
and so questioned her ancient mentors.

But these masterful ones,
        from their wiser view,
        had never found her behavior strange;
        they cherished her disruptions.

And counted as grace her propensity
        to ignite the fresh enlivening flame
        that rouses those who nap so deep
        they do not care to dream.

For wise ones know from ages past
        that till sleepers finally reconnect
        with their own great master plan,
        there can be no magic in their days
        nor lasting sparkle in their nights.

Someone must summon the winds of change
        to rearrange complacency
        and turn inertia to soulful action
        filled with conscious longing.

And the sages always meant, of course,
        for that someone to be her.

So now, when Fortune calls her name,
the Catalyst may sigh aloud
in profoundest human reluctance;

but she, nevertheless, accepts the task
to wrestle with the enmity
of those who in their secret hearts
    yearn to shake off
    the hypnotic trance
    imposed on them
    by a drowsy world
        that fears the soul
        on fire for life.

She lives to learn and love and teach,
    to see the once-dull animate,
    to feel the sudden surge of the few
        who catch the wave
        of her inspiration.

And then she knows her passion's reward,
    as they claim the birthright that is theirs,
    turn back to bid her a grateful farewell,
        and disappear
        bright-eyed for good
            over the horizon
            of their destiny.[14]

Chapter Thirteen

THE REALITY OF "BOTH/AND"

W hat does it mean to make the pain of grief your greatest ally? Seems like a tall order when your world has fallen apart and you are feeling blank, empty, exhausted and terribly, terribly sad.

In the midst of Stephen's illness, the answer to this question revealed a paradox and another question—Could I believe two opposite realities at the same time?

In other words, could I hold in mind not only what was wrong, but also what was right? Could I acknowledge not only what was gone, but also what remained and what was growing?

Even today, I must ask myself if I am willing to accept what is happening in the physical world as well as what is taking place at inner planes. My beloved was and is my teacher here.

Body and Soul Have Different Realities

One day when Stephen was approaching the last weeks of his life, he said to me, "My body is anxious because it knows that it's dying. And my soul is excited about where it's going."

These two realities were not abstract concepts to him. He was simultaneously experiencing both. He was grieving the impending loss of his physical life while rejoicing in the very real sense that his soul was going Home to a realm of light.

If we are attentive, we may notice the same paradoxical sensations going on within us when we have suffered a great

loss. Our human bodies experience the pain of physical separation that is very real in earth, though not at all real in heaven.

Life in this world is a dance of "both/and." Loss demands
our acknowledgement of this truth as does no other event.

When We Are Not There Yet

When someone is dying, the lead-up, passing and mourning of
that event are dramatically "both/and" situations. The gradual
decline of health, mobility or mental acuity are constant reminders that an end is on the horizon.

At some point, we know we will lose our darlings, so we
do our best to prepare. However, if we are not really there yet,
we do disservice to ourselves and our loved ones by anticipating
loss rather than abiding in the presence of life as it exists in this
moment.

Stephen and I worked very hard at not ruining today with
the probable sadness of tomorrow. In fact, I had a mantra that
I recited to myself over and over—"In this moment, everything
is alright." And everything was alright, until we reached a new
phase where it wasn't. When and how that phase arrived was
always a surprise anyway, so there was nothing to be gained by
anticipating the loss.

Attending to the Dark and the Light

I have observed that, for most people, coming to grips with the
paradox of life's natural cycles and inevitable endings is one of
their greatest challenges.

In conversations and workshops, I have found that people
who are pursuing a spiritual path often report the greatest difficulty. They will say things to me such as, "I shouldn't be grieving.
I know my loved one is in a better place. If I really do believe that,

why am I so sad? I feel like such a failure."

If they take this perspective to an extreme of refusing to grieve or acknowledge their deep feelings of loss, they may tip into what is called "spiritual bypass."[15] This is a term that means using spiritual practices as a way of glossing over or avoiding the messy aspects of emotion and psychology that loss of any kind presents.

Honoring the Totality of Experience

This is where my own experience can be helpful. I have been on a spiritual path for most of my life and I strive to maintain a spiritual perspective in all things. Yet when Stephen became ill, I felt guided—compelled, really—to go all the way into grieving the experiences as they progressed from his diagnosis, to advancing illness, to his death and to the absolute despair I felt when he was gone.

I spoke of having an amputated heart and it was over two years before I felt the Stephen-sized hole in my being truly beginning to heal. Still, somehow I knew that only by diving to the depths of grief's dark waters would I be able to touch bottom and push back up to the land of the living.

Honoring the totality of my experience of loss coupled with my spiritual beliefs and practice is what sheltered me there.

Chapter Fourteen

SPEAKING OF DEATH & DYING

Although times are changing, discussing death still carries the sense of a taboo, almost as if we fear that talking about the end of life will hasten our own. That superstition was never an issue in my childhood home.

Both of my parents grew up in a farming community where the cycles of birth and death were part of everyday life.

My father's older brother became a funeral director.

When we stayed with my grandparents in Missouri, we always visited the cemetery to place flowers on the graves of relatives—some long-gone and others more recently deceased.

At home in Denver, we frequently spent time with my mother's elderly aunt and uncle, and we knew many people of advanced years in our neighborhood and church.

In those early days, I attended a lot of funerals.

Setting the Tone for What Was to Come

Confronting the inescapable fact of death and its many implications can be frightening and confusing. It can revive distressing or even traumatic memories of loss, regret, disappointment, anger—the entire range of troubling human emotions. Still, if psychological health and emotional well-being are important to us, then discussing this most difficult of subjects is vital.

Stephen and I believed that talking about death and the dying process with open minds and hearts allowed us to set the tone for his transition—for our own well-being and that of our families who would be deeply affected by his leaving us.

Engaging in these conversations reinforced our faith in the continuity of life beyond this world. We shared our beliefs with friends and family in hopes that the strength of our convictions would comfort them. Perhaps our willingness to discuss our situation would offer a positive perspective into this most unwelcome subject.

We hoped that our way of being with each other as we faced Stephen's eventual passing would inspire others to accept his final act on the stage of life as a positive new beginning—not as a negative end.

Speaking of Denial

When I was conducting public workshops on end-of-life and palliative care issues for The Denver Hospice, I had occasion to hear from two individuals about the concept of denial. I began to see how casually the term is used these days and how careful we must be in ascribing the behavior to someone else.

The first comment came from the wife of an elderly man who was probably in the early stages of Alzheimer's.

"He seems to be in denial," she complained to me. "I can't get him to talk about his symptoms with me or his doctor. I just don't think he's accepting that his memory is getting worse."

The second comment was from a woman who was anxious about a friend. "How do you help someone who is in denial about her cancer?" she asked. "My friend was diagnosed six weeks ago and has gone downhill really quickly. I don't think she'll be here in another six weeks, and I just wish she could get to more of an accepting frame of mind."

The Problem with Our Opinions

At the time of these conversations, I did not have a ready response. They needed to talk and I needed to listen. As I considered their comments, I began to think that we may misread as denial what is only a preference for less expressive behavior.

I knew the older gentleman in the first example. When presented with dramatic loss, he had always been a man of few words. Even when a close family member died, he said very little. Sharing emotions or intimate personal details was not his style.

I was not acquainted with the woman who had cancer. But I do know that six weeks is a very short time to go from diagnosis to serene acceptance of one's rapidly approaching death. She could have been doing enormous amounts of internal processing that were too painful to share with anybody.

Could It Be Disbelief?

There is something so shockingly final about telling other people that we are terminally ill. I remember when Stephen and I first learned that his cancer was treatable but not curable, we were dumbstruck for a couple of days. We were not denying the diagnosis, but we found it very hard to believe that our lives had come to such a crossroads.

Finding the will and the strength to convey such terrible news to our families was one of the most difficult challenges we encountered. Each time we told the story made it more real—and that much more devastating. Wrapping our minds around the idea that this was not a bad dream from which we would gratefully awake took time.

Privacy Matters

Some years ago, I discovered by accident that a man who was

like a brother to me had just been diagnosed with double lung cancer. I shuddered when he said the report was "treatable, but not curable." He was still in shock over the news and was holding out hope for a miracle.

I hoped so, too, and asked what I could do for him and his wife. "Don't tell anyone," he said. "We're keeping this private."

Although I was aware that our wide circle of mutual friends would want to pray for him, I also understood his reluctance to deal with a lot of attention at such a delicate time.

Stephen's own desire for privacy was a matter I'd had to balance carefully. He was reticent to disclose his diagnosis. Still, I knew (and he agreed) that we needed the support and prayers of at least a few close companions who would walk with us as we braved this agonizing situation.

Surrendering Our Opinions About Death

Although Stephen's death was inspiring in many ways, I had to surrender my opinion that others could find similar peace at the end of their lives. Obviously, this is not possible in the case of sudden death. It is often not likely with a lengthy illness.

My mother's very painful and prolonged transition from this world disabused me of the idea that every death could be peaceful, let alone beautiful. She surprised me by being afraid to die. Because she was in so much pain, she decided she was not worthy of going to heaven. In her fear, she resisted dying for much longer than her hospice team or I thought possible.

We Can Be the Accepting Ones

Witnessing the suffering of another person is heart-wrenching. We also may suffer—especially if we do not agree with how they are dealing with the circumstances of their exit from this world.

One of the greatest gifts we can offer another person is our acceptance of their choices—even of their denial. Unless they explain their perspective, we cannot know exactly why they are not telling us about the details of their situation. I know there were aspects of Stephen's experience of dying that he did not confide in me.

People have their own reasons—privacy, disbelief or fear, embarrassment or guilt that they are letting us down by dying. If they do not choose to share this deeply personal process, it really is none of our business to label it.

These situations call us to do our own serious inner work and to relinquish our opinions that our loved ones should be walking their path in any way other than what they are able to do. Our greatest service is simply to be present with them.

We walk beside them as companions who do not judge. We attend, and that is enough.

If I Had Been Ill

Had I been the one with cancer, I doubt I would have chosen the aggressive treatment that Stephen did. For one thing, I was nowhere near as strong as he. I am sure my body would not have tolerated chemotherapy. Also, I had been through some frightening experiences with doctors when I was a child, so alternative therapies were always my first choice.

Nevertheless, this was Stephen's body and his decision. I had to surrender my fear of hospitals and be the advocate my husband needed and deserved.

The Battle Is Different for Each Person

We admire people who resist death. We do not want to see those we love giving up. Still, we understand that reaching a tipping point from fighting to stay alive to recognizing that the battle is over is different for each one. The difficulty of that process deserves our greatest compassion.

As social creatures, we humans are wired to affect each other emotionally. One of the most powerful ways in which we can be a positive presence for the dying is with our love and respect—and with our fearlessness.

To be respectful and quietly fearless while companioning another person through their suffering requires great courage. It is a stupendous gift. And it hurts. Nobody ever said it wouldn't.

Chapter Fifteen

ACROSS THE BRIDGE TO LOVE & JOY

Loss teaches us that the study of Love is a required course. No one is exempt. The exams are ongoing and most of them are pop quizzes. We may never feel fully prepared because the test is the lesson. The answer is a question. And the question is always the same—How well did you love in this situation?

The experience of loss can illustrate how Love manifests in grief. How the process unfolds day by day. How grief teaches as it purges. How it prepares us for the next lessons of Love.

Grief helps create the bridge from our old life to the new one that must be allowed to emerge. We stand on that connector, looking into the depths of our experience—seeing reflected back an image of our self we do not quite recognize.

We Are Strangers on the Span

Loss can make us alien to ourselves and to others. It compels us to let go of who and what we have loved. Of who and what we thought we were. Of expectations of who and what we may become. In order to heal, we must release all of those images back into the stream.

On the bridge of grief, we learn to rest in surrender.

Ultimately, Love desires to call us across to joy's luminescence. In that understanding, we learn that grieving can be a merciful process—even when it overwhelms us.

We gaze once again into the emotional waters and see that

our image is always letting go. Always fluid. Always in love. The reflections are life's ripples. We study them in our own laboratory of being. Then we let them go and cross over grief's bridge to the holy precincts of our heart.

How Much Love Have You Let in Today?

I once heard that question asked by a long-time student of the mystical traditions of East and West. Hearing this man speak was like perceiving myriad streams of universal wisdom swirling together to create a complex river of enlightenment, inner strength and profound compassion.

He had also walked the path of loss and grief. He had drunk from the deep waters of bereavement and learned to taste of their sweet transformative powers. Listening to him was like hearing my own life narrated back to me. And his question, "How much love have you let in today?" cracked me wide open.

How much, indeed? At the moment, I was feeling more anxious than loving. Distressed by the medical condition that was causing my elderly mother great discomfort and frustration. And tired of feeling that everything happening in my life was about me taking care of other people's needs.

So, no, I was not letting in much love at all. The man's words slammed me up against a serious piece of a shadow self that I am not sure I had ever really noticed.

Will We Receive Life's Offer of Love?

I have always been good at giving—a skill I learned from being on stage as a singer and musical comedy actress where the show must go on, no matter how you feel.

The same applies to restaurant work—an industry that employs a lot of actors. I recently had a conversation with an actor-waiter who served me lunch. I asked him if he had ever noticed the similarity between theatre and food service. He laughed and agreed that a lunch or dinner rush can be like "show time." You give your all, no matter what.

The challenge is that while giving your all is admirable, being a chronic "giver" can also be a way to control, to cope, to not be vulnerable or receptive.

Therein lies the challenge.

Before Love can wedge a toe past this psychological gatekeeper, we must decide that we are worthy of receiving as much as we give. Do we appreciate the special qualities that make us uniquely lovable? Or do we see only blemishes, imperfections, flaws or failures to live up to some impossibly perfect self-image?

It may be more blessed to give than to receive. Yet, if we fail to receive what others affectionately offer us, the circle of blessing is incomplete.

The heart's door must swing both ways if we are to truly love—if we are to live life in the fullness that a generous Universe longs to give.

Grief's Question About Love

As we step onto the bridge that leads from loss through grief to joy, we ponder grief's question:

> Will you accept my love, knowing that it will strip you of your defenses, render you more vulnerable than you believe you can bear and ultimately transform you into more of your divine reality than you ever imagined? Will you accept the idea that love and joy are waiting on the Other Side of the bridge?

This is one of life's hardest and potentially most rewarding lessons—when we summon the courage to endure the trials of loss and accept that joy lives concealed in grief.

Discovering My Own Ground

My grief has been dramatically transformed, yet what has taken its place? When I ask that question, a vivid memory comes to mind of an unusual connection with my husband.

I am remembering our vacation in Hawaii. We had joined my parents for a week on Oahu, and then the two of us spent a couple of days by ourselves on Maui where we went snorkeling.

I have never been a strong swimmer. Despite the gloriously clear water, I was afraid to put my face all the way in because I instantly lost all sense of where I was—except in this vast ocean where I was unmoored.

However, if I held on to the waistband of Stephen's swim trunks as we paddled along, I was anchored enough to look into the fabulous underwater world where exquisite, multi-hued sea life greeted my amazed eyes.

Anchoring is what Stephen did for me in many ways while he was alive. He grounded me in his reality so I could find my own. When he died, I genuinely despaired that I would become completely disconnected from safe harbor.

As time and self-discovery have progressed, I have found a way to my own grounding that is now raising me up to a practical spirituality that reaches deep into the earth and high into the etheric. This is what I used to catch sight of Stephen doing. Now, when I decide to welcome the ambiguity of another transition, I can do it, too.

Chapter Sixteen

REFLECTIONS ON GIVING CARE

I have often thought that the caregiver's role in life's transitions must have been what the Psalmist meant by the valley of the shadow of death—as a dark night casts its pall while we must continue putting one foot in front of the other.

This valley can also be one of light—as the radiance of the Other Side impinges on the consciousness of the person who is dying. Stephen and I experienced how that light can unite caregiver and patient in a holy alliance that is beyond the human capacity of either one.

The Grace of Hearts United

Shortly before Stephen died, I told him that I would not have chosen to be anywhere other than by his side as he endured the greatest trial of his life. I really did feel that caring for him was a holy honor that I would not have missed for the world.

I do not know that I could have said that to anybody else. Stephen was and is my soul's other half and that made all the difference. In ways I am sure I do not fully understand, the deep love we shared as twin flames walking a spiritual path gave us the strength and courage to face his death with hearts united.

We were in complete accord in our conviction that we were going through a spiritual initiation. We knew our souls were being tested. This trial by fire was the fulfillment of a promise we had made before this lifetime.

At the time of his illness, we did not know that our perspective might be considered unusual. I know now it was a grace.

We Need Not Be Perfect to Care

Even with our unwavering determination to fulfill the promise
of our love, as physical challenges increased for both of us, I was
often not able to provide the level of care I would have preferred.

Of course, I did my best to be sensitive to Stephen's
needs and he did his best to help me meet those needs. In those
moments, we loved, we learned and we moved on without the
benefit of hindsight that comes with time and maturity.

Perhaps the most important lesson I learned is that we
need not be perfect to offer care. Developing a more compassionate attitude toward myself reduced my stress and improved my
caring for Stephen.

Ultimately, there are no hard-and-fast rules, only our
attunement. In that light, I am offering the following reflections
as a meditation on how caregiving might be approached as a
spiritual journey to the heart of compassion.

At the Heart of Care

Compassionate caregiving arises from an open heart. It comes
from a heart that befriends itself, one that perceives itself honestly, one that pays attention to what is arising in the moment
without judging it as right or wrong.

The compassionate heart is engaged, fully in contact with
the pain of the other person and yet, not overcome by that pain.
This is a heart that has been purged of pettiness and the materi-
alism that tries to keep us earth-bound when our soul longs to
soar to dimensions of higher consciousness.

The Dying Also Have Gifts to Give

When we can enter into the caregiving process in a spirit of what we are receiving, rather than how much we are giving or what we are losing, we may find our service being perfected.

There is an alchemy that happens when we offer care from an open heart. The dying also have gifts to give if we are not too burdened by our own sorrow to receive the joy that is just across the way.

The one who gives care becomes the one who receives blessing from the heart of the one to whom care is given. Both giver and receiver are transformed. Here is selfless service that is free of disappointment, resentment or anger at the patient who is no longer the person we once knew.

A Holy Honor

The heart-centered caregiver becomes a conduit for universal healing. If we can approach our duties as a privilege, the quality of our service is transformed, and we are elevated in the process.

"Inasmuch as ye have done it unto the least of these my brethren, ye have done it unto me" becomes our view of service when seen through the eyes of compassion. It is a holy honor that returns to us much more than it takes away.

Unfortunately, not everyone shares this perspective. A woman at one of my workshops said, "You just get through the death. If you can find meaning later, good for you."

I felt sad for her and for the many people who do go through really terrible experiences with death. And yet, by merely gritting our teeth and powering through, we may miss a potential blessing the Divine has secreted away in the dying process.

If both caregiver and patient can enter into the extraordinary challenges of facing death together, they may share a glimpse of the heavenly realms that hover over these final hours.

We can refine our ability to accept this vision by opening our hearts rather than steeling them against unpleasantness, sadness, anger, pain and the loss we know is coming.

Realizing We Are Not Alone

Even when we are in great pain, feeling most desperately isolated and abandoned, we are not alone. We are part of the human family that suffers. "Other people feel this," we can say to ourselves.

We imagine that in this very moment there are countless other human beings around the world who are enduring the exact process of losing a loved one or their own lives.

Our perception widens. That part of us which was focused on our own suffering now chooses to witness other faces as sad as ours, other eyes brimming with tears, other hearts broken in grief, other loved ones struggling for release from pain.

In this moment of shared humanity, we are no longer disturbed or shocked by the suffering of others. We feel it with them. We are they, and they are the same as we are.

Sending Out Love and Light

A powerful loving-kindness wells up within our own fractured hearts and we say aloud, "May all be free from suffering."

We send out to others the love and light that we know will ease their pain because it is what we also need. When we experience this heart-felt compassion within the depths of our soul, in that moment of exquisite love, we are comforted.

As I embraced the difficulties of Stephen's final weeks of life as opportunities to send prayers of comfort to others who were suffering, as well as to my darling, my entire being grew stronger. And my heart softened.

I did not so reactively brace against pain. Although lack of sleep and the need for constant vigilance were exhausting, the care I gave no longer tended to burn me out. Instead, it buoyed me up—even as my heart was breaking. The feelings of sorrow continued to arise, but I was able to stay with them—allowing them to turn into gratitude and peace, and to transform me in the process.

A Gift of Transfiguration

Giving care can increase our self-knowledge. As we strive to summon deep reservoirs of strength and sensitivity, we may discover resistances to myriad aspects of the human condition. Inner guidance brings those resistances to our attention so we can transmute them.

We may begin to realize a sensitivity to the soul's innate beauty that death's visage cannot obscure. When we enter fully into the opportunity to give care, we may experience the transfiguration of our loved ones as well as ourselves.

I once read a quote from Sufi mystics stating that it is the nature of the Divine to desire manifestation. If that is true, then whoever we are tending wears the body of God. That body has been extended to us in its affliction so we may learn to see the beauty within and to love with a purer love.

Stephen never ceased to be beautiful to me, even as his body weakened and began showing the haggard appearance of the cancer that would take him. A week before his death an event occurred that was a genuine transfiguration.

That evening, Stephen felt strong enough to bathe with me helping. He was still able to hold on to the shower rod and stand for me to towel him off. As I knelt to dry his feet and legs, I was reminded of a ritual we used to perform at our church to commemorate Jesus's washing the feet of his disciples.

Suddenly, the image of Stephen's body became numinous. I was not only ministering to my husband. For an instant, I was certain that if I looked up, I would see the face of Jesus. These were legs of the Master himself. This was the body of Christ and I felt that my service would be a holy one if I could maintain that awareness.[16]

What Is Lost? What Is Gained?

So, I ask myself—If Stephen had not lost his life, would I have discovered the abiding presence of appreciation that I now feel for mine?

Perhaps. Perhaps not. I do know for certain that, inspired by Stephen's spiritual presence, I have forged a new life from our love. And as he continues to share the illumination he is attaining on the Other Side, I discover deeper understanding of what is most real in me. More than thirteen years ago, I thought I had lost everything that mattered. Now I know I have gained much more.

PART FOUR

Embracing Life's Final Journey

Joy lands where it will
and joins us
to its effervescent flow
that banishes all sense
of separation.

Chapter Seventeen

Living Well, Dying Well

One of my favorite statements about the end of life says, We die well because we have lived well; and we live well because we know that we will die.

Irish poet, priest and philosopher John O'Donohue says we are born with death as our companion through life. But we moderns try to ignore that fact by hiding the dying away in nursing homes and hospitals. So, how do we die well if we refuse to admit that the end will come to all? First, we live well.

Living Well in Service

In their inspiring collaboration, *The Book of Joy,*[17] His Holiness the Dalai Lama and the late Archbishop Desmond Tutu define living well as developing loving-kindness and compassion through concern for the well-being of others.

They suggest that our self-care be done without ego or pride or grasping for rewards. Rather, they encourage us to maintain a healthy body, mind and spirit in order to be of service to others—which may continue until the hour of our own death.

I saw this in Stephen's last days. Being the private person he was, his preference would have been to disappear into a cave and simply merge with the elements. He did manage to die a very private death by waiting until I had gone to sleep before he slipped away. In the meantime, he recognized how acutely his family needed to see him.

"This is service," he said to me one day when his parents and an aunt and uncle who were visiting from out of state were on their way to our house. During the hour we were together, the two of us did our best to comfort these dear ones who had come to comfort us.

I often experienced this same conundrum after Stephen was gone. People did not know what to say to me. I could see they were uncomfortable commenting on the fact that my husband had died. So, I told them stories about some of our inspiring experiences. My sharing with them opened the door for them to share with me, and we all received the love and support we needed.

The Need for a Helping Hand

Crossing over seems to want companionship. A soul taking that final step may need a helping hand and a smile of welcome from the Other Side.

When my mother was desperately afraid to let go of this life, I got the distinct and rather troubling impression that she wanted me to go with her. Instead, I encouraged her to take the hand of her deceased son-in-law whom she trusted, and I begged Stephen to extend his hand to her. Apparently they agreed, because she died the next day, which was his birthday.

Once my mother reached the Other Side, I know she was greeted by familiar faces and tender embraces. Not long after her passing, I had a vision of her tending roses in a beautiful garden, just as she had done in life.

When Fear of Death Departs

One of the surprising implications of the near-death experience (NDE) is that consciousness appears not to reside in the brain.

During the time those going through an NDE are clinically dead, they show no brain activity on operating room monitors. Yet, they later report that their awareness continued as their soul lifted out of their body. For a brief period, many watched and heard what was going on in the hospital and then they went on a journey into ethereal realms.

Communication with guides who accompanied them was conducted telepathically. Travel between scenes like an unspeakably beautiful garden or intergalactic dimensions was instantaneous. At some point, the patients were told by their guides that they must return to life. They reluctantly accepted that decision and soon found themselves back in their bodies—to the great surprise of the doctors who had been urgently tending their "deceased" patients for several minutes.

A person's recollection of their NDE often remains as vivid as the day it occurred. One of the most common effects of the experience is that the fear of death has departed.

Learning Never Stops

NDEs and grief have a lot in common. Both experiences open a window into new dimensions of perception. I would like to imagine that the extremes which cause these circumstances are not necessary, yet it appears that they are. At least for most of us.

The habit patterns of even the most selfless lives can become calcified. Spirit may be the only force in the Universe that continually makes all things new. So, the imperfections of earthly life oblige and collaborate with the wisdom of the Divine to shock us awake to the need for change.

In those moments, life urges us to adopt a spaciousness toward the possibility of soul growth. We are encouraged to continue developing compassion, wisdom and strength of character.

Until we take leave of this planet, we live well by learning well. My communion with Stephen's spirit tells me that learning also never stops on the Other Side.

More Thoughts on Living Well

To live well is to be in touch with the invisible world of our origin, which is both source and goal—where we have been and where we are going. Life remains vibrant and keen with a knife-edge of clarity when we live in the simultaneous awareness of origin and destiny.

Knowing we are bookended in the fullness of light on both sides of the veil keeps us fresh. Taking nothing for granted, we honor the fragility of our earthly existence as well as the immense power of the divine spark in our heart which animates us body, mind, soul and spirit.

We are both seen and unseen—to ourselves and to those around us. Accepting how much of us is invisible vivifies the tangible space we dwell within and opens our desire to penetrate the veiled mysteries of being.

A life vigorously well-lived invites those mysteries into the physical. In the process we are aware that our very atoms, cells and electrons are being pulled into celestial dimensions. Day by day, a well-lived life etherealizes until we enter the invisible realm that lights our heart for eternity.

Living well encompasses the length and breadth of our search for meaning and purpose. Loss and grief accelerate the process. Dying well completes it.

A Beautiful Death

A colleague once told me, "If you ever have an opportunity to be with a loved one who is dying, welcome the experience."

I have always been glad for that advice because those few words set me on a course of profound inquiry into the mystery of life that occurs when it ends.

When my father became terminally ill with the lung disease that had burdened him for decades, I did not hesitate to be with him in the hospital as he completed his exit from this world.

I have often wished I had known then the details of the dying process that I have since lived through and studied. Still, my father's passing gave me such a rich, unfiltered window into a soul's process of crossing the bridge to the next world, perhaps my lack of knowledge was the way things were meant to be.

"Did Anything Go Wrong?"

My mother told me about an event that occurred one evening when I had returned to their house to rest. These two sweet-hearts, who had been married for over fifty-seven years, were talking about the adventures they had shared since meeting at a church ice cream social in the small town of Lebanon, Missouri.

My mother said to my father, "We'll just remember the good things, not the things that went wrong." He looked at her and said in all sincerity, "Did anything go wrong?"

How I wish we all could come to a place of such profound gratitude for life's challenges and with a heart full of such deep forgiveness. Then, at the end of our days, we could declare that, really, nothing less than love ever happened.

Celestial Greetings

Not long after their conversation, my father slipped into a coma, and the veil between worlds began to thin. While my mother and I watched at his bedside, he eagerly reached up to a corner of the ceiling of his hospital room.

He had been very weak, but now his arms remained raised for several minutes. He was gesturing and smiling and moving his mouth as if he were speaking with someone he was delighted to meet as they came to greet him.

A few hours later, when his soul did eventually take flight, his eighty-one-year-old face became smooth, almost translucent, and graced with a smile that I can only describe as cherubic.

That image remained in my heart as a gift of inspiration and hope throughout the journey with loss that Stephen and I walked together ten years later.

Chapter Eighteen

"I Will Be There Tomorrow Night"

Stories that offer a picture of the Other Side are some of the most important we can share—for inspiration and for the hope they offer us about dying well.

The following letter is from 1875. It was written by my great-great grandfather, William Lafferty, to his family in Bedford, Pennsylvania, telling of the death of his wife, Margaret. She passed away at the age of fifty-six in Missouri where she, her husband and other family members had moved some years earlier.

My father found this letter among family treasures which his mother had been saving. Its quaint language and vivid descriptions helped inspire him to research the Lafferty family genealogy. I wonder if this story might also have inspired the beauty of his own passing.

I am grateful to share this touching example of someone who is stepping into the heaven world while offering her family a glimpse of that radiant destination before her soul takes flight.

December 14, 1875
Oakland Post Office, Laclede County, Missouri

Dear Mother, Brother John and Sister Barbara,

It is with a grief-stricken heart that I write to you once more for I have sad news to tell you of the death of my dear wife.

She took sick in mid-September and kept getting worse all the time. The Doctor gave her some relief at times and she lived on till the 19th of November.

She was only confined to bed half the time. She could sit or walk around the house by steadying herself till about two hours before she died and her voice never failed her until two hours before death. She told Sarah several days before her death that she should not weep for her, that she was not going to die yet and that she would tell her when she was going to die.

The night before her death, sitting by the fire on a chair and leaning back, she fell asleep and began to quote the Scripture in her sleep. A neighbor woman became alarmed and woke her before I could get to her, but I said to let her alone that she was not any worse.

On waking, she said her sleep was so sweet that she could have slept a hundred years and was getting ready to sing when she was awakened. When we later got her up and sat her in her chair again, she told me if she went to sleep for a month I should not let them wake her up. She was sound asleep in 15 minutes and commenced singing some of the New Testament and every word and line sounded like poetry or a Hymn.

After an hour or longer and still asleep, she said, "I can't sing any more tonight, but I will be there tomorrow night," repeating several times, "I will be there tomorrow night." When awake she said things were brighter than pure gold.

She told me the next morning that she had seen all she wanted to see. I asked what she saw; she said there was nothing there but what was pure, just and holy.

So on the morning of the 19th, about 10:00 o'clock, I think she was struck with death and she called the children all up to her bed and told them she was going to leave them; that she had done a mother's duty by them all, and that she now wanted them all to prepare to meet her in Heaven and exhorted them for some length of time. Then she turned to Ivey last, telling her to be a good child and meet her in Heaven.

She said she would like to live with them a few years longer, at least 10 years, because we had moved so far and were among strangers. She said her mind was as bright as the noonday sun; and she lived until 6:30 o'clock, November 19, when the breath left her.

Well, dear Mother, I have given you a small sketch of the last words of my dear wife, but I could tell you more if I could see you. We buried her in a black walnut coffin, well finished, lined inside and covered outside.

Her funeral was preached by a good old Methodist preacher, using First Corinthians 15th chapter and part of 52 verse "for the trumpet shall sound and the dead shall be raised incorruptible and we shall be changed" and all the 23rd Psalm was read.

I will give you her age, 56 years 7 months and 20 days. But I am satisfied that she is with the glorious millions above and will never return to me any more, but it won't be very long till I will go to her and we will part no more.

O Mother, I feel so lonesome but I think we can get along very well as long as Sarah stays with me. She is now going on 19 and nobody has raised any better child than her; it almost broke her heart to part with her mother. She has never given myself nor her mother one ill word in all her life nor has never went to any parties nor frollicks and I trust never will.

Yours truly until death,

(signed) *Wm Lafferty*

[He lived another 21 years.]

Chapter Nineteen

THE SHARED DEATH EXPERIENCE

During the time I was presenting public workshops for the educational arm of The Denver Hospice, I was a member of ADEC.[18] The Association of Death Educators and Counselors is an international organization comprised of academics, medical and non-medical hospice personnel, chaplains, counselors and therapists whose goal is to promote understanding, compassion and best practices in the care of the dying and grieving.

At one of their national conferences, I met Lizzy Miles, a young woman who had just published her book[19] about the incredible experiences she and two female cousins had shared as their Aunt Jerry was in the process of leaving this world.

I was fascinated to hear Lizzy talk about seeing images of her aunt's life review, visions of deceased relatives who had gathered on the Other Side to welcome Jerry as she crossed over and sensations that Lizzy knew were those of her aunt, not her own.

Her story confirmed that the veil between worlds thins when a person is in the process of crossing over. She also affirmed that if we are sensitive and attentive, we may witness their ethe-realization—almost as participants.

Before meeting Lizzy, I had not known of a term for these events. From her, I learned that *Life After Life* author and NDE researcher, Raymond Moody, had labeled such phenomena as the "shared death experience."[20]

Much of what Lizzy described resonated with me because

I had shared a similar experience with Stephen. Three days before his passing, he saw something on the inner that he needed my help to understand. Here is how this extraordinary event unfolded.

What Do the Signs Say?

Stephen was very restless tonight. Even with anti-anxiety medication, he was up and down, sitting on the side of the bed and talking to me intently.

"Are we going back to the USA now?" he asked.

"Yes, we're going home," I offered.

"Are we flying?" he asked, a bit eagerly.

"Yes." It was easy to imagine being airborne.

At one point, he said, "Did we do anything wrong?" He seemed concerned that we were somehow in trouble. A couple of days earlier, he had asked if the police were involved. At that time, he was conscious of being in two worlds and just needed clarification. Tonight, he was fully in the dream world.

"No, we did everything right," I assured him. "That's why we're free."

"Do we have an escort?"

"Yes, they're called Blue Angels. They're F-16 fighter planes." I was out on a limb here, but that's the first thing that popped into my head; so I went with it.

"That's a hell of an escort."

"Honey, it was a hell of a battle." I was not exaggerating!

That explanation seemed to satisfy Stephen and he went back to sleep for a couple of hours. Around 4:00 a.m. he sat up again. I was sleeping with our bed pushed over next to his hospital bed so we could snuggle if he wanted to be touched, and so I could easily check to see if he was breathing.

However, when he decided to swing his legs out of his bed, I had to leap out on the other side of mine and run around to where he was sitting so he didn't fall on the floor. This time his questioning was more insistent.

"What do the signs say?"

I really was at a loss here, so I said, "I can't see them, but I think they say *Home* or perhaps *This Way to Paradise.*"

Then he said, "Dance with me." He was trying to hold me and stand up. Now, this was comical, because the only other time we had danced in eighteen years of marriage was at our wedding. Stephen was many things, but he was not a dancer.

"Let me just hold you and we'll dance right here," I said, swaying back and forth as I tried to keep him seated.

"No, turn around. Tell me what the signs say."

He took my shoulders and with amazing force turned me around so I was facing in the same direction as he was. But, of course, I still couldn't see any signs.

"Honey, I can't tell, but I'm almost sure they say something about Home." I felt bad that he was so frustrated. For some time, he had not been able to read with his physical eyes. Now his dream eyes were failing him as well and he needed help that I could not give.

I had been reading to him from his favorite books. But now, when there was an important message for him from the Other Side, I didn't have access to it. I tried to reassure him, but I felt sad that I was failing him at this critical time.

Somewhat reluctantly, he agreed to go back to sleep, so I tucked him in and returned to my side of the bed. As soon as my head hit the pillow and I closed my eyes, I saw the signs! Dozens of them, held up like placards by all kinds of smiling people—young, old, large, small. And, judging by the varied appearance of their clothes, they were from different periods in history.

In big, bold letters the signs said:

WELCOME
STEPHEN ECKL!

"Honey!" I exclaimed. "I see the signs! They say, *Welcome Stephen Eckl!* They know you and they have the welcoming committee out for you!"

"You mean like Ellis Island?"

"Yes, but this is better than Ellis Island. It's much more beautiful and here they know your name. And they're all ready to welcome you."

That seemed to be the answer he was looking for. He immediately settled down and slept soundly until morning and he rested peacefully throughout the day on Monday.

How interesting, I thought as I nestled back into bed that night. Stephen is following the metaphor of going to the USA, the land of freedom, with a stop at Ellis Island, the reception station for people coming to the New World—exactly where he is going![21]

Chapter Twenty

IN THE MOMENTS OF PASSING

As I was preparing these chapters about embracing life's final journey, a member of my church was at home in hospice care. He was expected to make his transition very soon.

I could easily imagine him being lovingly tended and made as comfortable as possible. Hospice nurses are particularly skilled at helping a patient's body relax into its passing so the soul can take flight to its next destination.

What a sacred time this is—when a soul is fully engaged in doing its final work on earth in preparation for the journey home. The image comes to mind of "unpacking" for this trip. Of divesting one's self of all that is less than the light the soul has accrued.

The soul's longing for higher realms can be very strong in these final days or hours. Still, active dying is a process that may take some time. There are signs, of course, but hospice nurses are reluctant to say exactly how long the leave-taking will require. Each passing is unique.

Attending in the Final Hours

A smooth passing depends on keeping the patient free from pain or disturbance. The body is very wise in its ability to close down its earthly functions. As it goes about this business, it needs to be honored and tended with the care we would give to a vulnerable, newborn baby.

The soul truly is being born into a new life—just beyond

the veils of time, from the world of the seen to the world of the Unseen. The process is one of life's great mysteries.

Sometimes a patient will rally—making those at the bedside think perhaps death is not as close as they imagined. They may decide this is a good time to step away and get something to eat or take a rest. Keeping vigil can be exhausting when the person's active dying is not progressing as quickly as expected.

I remember crying out to God, "Why can't my Daddy just die!" He was obviously eager to go, and we were praying for him to be released from the labored breathing of the lung disease that was taking him. But, of course, only God knows the timing of our exit. Our job is not to hasten that event; only to attend.

Our Most Intimate Experience

Dying is perhaps the most intimate experience we may have in this life. Sometimes the dying person will slip away when they are only briefly alone. Despite Stephen's hospital bed being pulled up adjacent to our bed where I was sleeping, he still managed to silently take his leave.

Although he had been in a coma for about twenty-four hours, around 12:30 a.m. I heard him call my name, waking me from sleep. He remained unconscious, and I could see that he was still breathing. He did not appear to be in any pain.

I lay there for a few minutes, watching him and listening. When I heard nothing else, I dozed off. Then at exactly 1:11 a.m. I abruptly woke up and Stephen was gone.

Creating an Environment of Beauty and Peace

Most people say they would prefer to die at home, in familiar surroundings, with loved ones present. Sometimes that is not possible. Still, hospice nurses and others who attend the dying know that Spirit takes care of souls who are going Home.

Books such as *Final Gifts*[22] or *Visions, Trips and Crowded Rooms*[23] offer inspiring examples of how the final moment of transition is well-attended from the Other Side, even if outer circumstances are not optimal. This is the moment when previously departed loved ones may appear with angels, masters and other spirit beings to welcome the soul to the glorious realm that has been calling them.

I remember Stephen saying that he saw "friendly guys coming up the path" toward him. He knew he would not be alone when his soul took that last step.

In the Final Moments

Even with a beautiful death, leaving this world is not easy. For some, crossing over can be a painful, sorrowful or fearful experience. In the days of COVID, many of our sweethearts have died in isolation without the comfort of human presence or touch. This has been the source of enormous grief to family and friends who were not allowed to attend their loved ones' final hours.

Regardless of circumstances, we do our best to create an atmosphere of peace, honor, safety—and respect for the person's desires for how they would like to take leave of this world.

Until souls finally cross over, reaching their destination can feel like an enormous step into the vast Unknown. Depending on their faith tradition, or lack of one, facing this eventuality can be daunting. Any comfort we can bring to another's doubts or fears about their imminent passing is a service well-rendered.

Chapter Twenty-One

BECOMING THE BOAT

Where do we go when we die? Is there an afterlife or do we merely disappear into oblivion? Are we met with an eternity of love or judgment?

Who is the "I" that makes the transition from this dimension to the next? What part of me (if any) goes on to another existence in the invisible realm? How do I reach the Promised Land?

Stephen deeply pondered these questions. He felt strongly that spiritual practice functions like a wisdom boat that carries us over life's rough waters. When we journey from one harbor to the next, we are meant to arrive safe and secure, and blessed with greater understanding of our own path through life.

We may employ many "boats" before our final crossing. The key is for each new vessel to take us closer to our inner reality than its predecessor.

Sailing into Our Final Hours

Stephen believed we are supposed to become the boat ourselves. We are meant to have internalized Spirit's lessons so completely that we sail into our final hours on the majestic ship of a resplendent, genuine Self. Here is how he explained it to me:

The process is for us to become our own Noah's Ark.
We build it by hand—board by board, plank by plank—

gathering in the spiritual resources our soul will need
to survive after the physical body drops away. If we are
fortunate to live to an advanced age before it rains, we
will have constructed a mighty vessel.

Will My Boat Float?

Of course, we do not expect to live as long as Noah, and sometimes the thunder booms and the lightning strikes before we
barely have the boat's hull in place. So, what do we do?

Being with Stephen throughout his dying process taught
me that every day we must ask ourselves—If the rains came
today, would my boat float? Although I may not consider myself
particularly enlightened, what "spirit stuff" have I gathered into
my ark that will go with me to the far-distant shore?

Weaving a Garment of Light

Another way to think of becoming the boat is the idea of weaving an ethereal garment of light. Thread by lustrous thread, this
wedding garment or deathless solar body is created from our
devotions, prayers, service and spiritual communion.

Whether or not we and our twin flame have been called to
an ongoing mission beyond the grave, our souls are destined to
continue learning and growing far beyond this incarnation. In or
out of embodiment, life is meant to spiral ever-upward in vibration to a more refined realization of Self.

Where twin flames are involved, we know that our actions
directly affect the ability of both our souls to increase in wisdom
and in love from here to eternity.

The garment of light is the accrued spiritual substance we
have garnered. It is a manifestation of our attainment. When
divinely ordained, it is through this energetic forcefield that our

souls are able to connect after one of us dies.

We do not force the connection through human willing or wishing. Doing so can cause harm to both souls, even if communion after death is part of our mission. By focusing on garnering more light, we ensure our alignment with Divine Will, and we clear the way for an ongoing relationship with our beloved.

A Compelling Synergy

Our garment of light will be unique to us individually. And yet, because we and our twin flame were created from the same soul blueprint, a compelling synergy will inextricably draw us together.

Here we will meet in our finer bodies in a deeper, stronger, more vital love that is free of affect or psychology, though not of our soul essence. As our love grows, our communion will become richer, more vibrant and of greater effectiveness in whatever service we are called to perform.

Gratitude Builds Boats and Bridges

In addition to becoming the wisdom boat that carries us to the shores of new life after loss, we are also called to build bridges of connection between ourselves and those to whom we offer comfort and care.

Perhaps the most important bridge we build is the one that spans the visible world we inhabit and the invisible one we seek. Adopting an attitude of gratitude creates blessings of mind and heart that can do exactly that.

For Stephen and me, being grateful for dark nights as well as sunny days has been key to our embracing the mystical journey of self-discovery that carries us forward in joy.

A Prayer for Gratitude

May we be grateful to possess
hearts that can grieve,
that can feel and express the love
for our dear ones,

which perhaps in their absence
seems it has no place to go—
and yet can now be sent out
to a world in need,
as a legacy of the connection we shared.

May we be grateful that our love
which was personal
can now be universal.

May we be grateful for the blessings
of a greater presence of light and love and joy
that grief opens before us and in us.

And may we be grateful
for the continuity of life
which one day will carry us
in the joyful boat we have become
to an awareness of the majesty of Divine Love
that is, in reality, as close as breath.

PART FIVE

Holding On
and
Letting Go

When joy fills us up
with its perfect essence,
we feel whole, complete
and ecstatically real.

Chapter Twenty-Two

HOW HOLDING ON CAN HELP

When Stephen took off for realms of light, I did not imme-diately launch into letting go of the past. My days were consumed with the grief I was experiencing in the present.

For a long time, grief also comprised my future as I worked to integrate the past we had shared with the new relationship we were both exploring on opposite sides of the boundary between worlds. What I did commence mere days after his passing was a process that remains ongoing, even thirteen years after that heart-wrenching event.

Actually, it's called living.

Life really is all about change. Sometimes that means releasing things that no longer fit with our current reality. It also means letting go of people who are finished here.

Upon reflection, however, I think it is much healthier not to think about letting go at all. Forcing yourself to release what is not complete can cause your grief to become complicated—emo-tionally or psychologically damaging.

One Woman's Courage

When I attended a workshop on "Death as a Spiritual Teacher," I clearly saw the wisdom of giving ourselves time to let go. There were about twenty-five people in the group and most of them were experiencing the deep pain of recent and dramatic loss.

One woman had lost her husband, her father, her cat and

her job in the previous three months. She had also moved from out of state during the same period of time.

I still cannot fathom how she was functioning after so much loss. She was concentrating on simply taking one painful step at a time. I found her courage breathtaking. She knew she needed support and had sought out a group of compassionate strangers to hold her in a safe space of unconditional acceptance while she just breathed.

When I observed these dear souls in the workshop dealing with the abject pain I remembered so well, I was convinced that holding on can be at least as important as letting go. Especially if we can think of holding as cherishing what still exists rather than clutching at what was.

What Exactly Do We Hold?

In the early days of loss, I held many things. Or perhaps they held me. Photos of Stephen and me together. The precious portrait an artist created for his memorial service. Some of his clothes. His woodworking equipment. His books.

I kept many items that he had touched and used and loved. I held them because they created a sort of scaffolding to support my grieving as it unfolded. These treasures gently reminded me of ways in which Stephen grounded me.

By holding them in honor and love, I learned which pos-sessions were necessary for my new life and which were not. The items that I could not use fell away on their own. As more exter-nals let me go, I simplified my life and eventually allowed room for fresh complexity as new treasures took the place of old ones.

The process was natural, unhurried and kind. I think if I had immediately tried to release Stephen's possessions, I would have broken into a thousand pieces. Instead, I focused on not letting go too soon.

I let Nature take its course. And it did in its own mysterious way that held me in the embrace of that benign spirit—my Wise Inner Counselor—who knows me and my needs extremely well. I began to feel solid from the inside-out.

Embracing the Way Ahead

When a loved one dies, we lose a certain innocence, especially if their dying is our first experience with death. We grow old over night. The sheer enormity of absence can overwhelm us. The only thing we know for certain is that we and life will never be the same.

Dramatic loss is an assault on all our senses. No part of us escapes. The way ahead can seem like a mountain too high, a path too rough, a river too deep and wide. And yet, we must keep going.

Holding Our Inner Child

In the midst of loss's complexities, grief has a tendency to reduce our capacity for complex thinking. We may feel ourselves functioning with the simplicity and vulnerability of a child. The world we had previously mastered is now foreign, confusing and too vast for us to handle.

Part of us just wants somebody to make us a cup of hot cocoa, put us to bed and read us a story with a happy ending. We long for a grown-up who understands our internal devastation to take us by the hand and lead us back into the sunshine.

Of course, the reality is that we ourselves must become that grown-up. In the meantime, what if we were to approach our situation with the curiosity of a child? What if we adopted a sense of wonder that someone we dearly loved has gone on to another world that is filled with ethereal beauty and mysteries which we ourselves may discover one day?

Many children do see into realms of light and joy. Given an opportunity and encouraged by the adults in their lives, they will use their natural creativity to explore their experience.

We can be that loving adult to the child within us who needs reassurance and a way of passing through the difficulties loss presents—to achieve what seems impossible at first.

Focusing on Self-Care

One way I eventually learned to support my inner child was by conserving my energy. I discovered situations that I did not want to be involved in. I gave myself permission to say "no" to social activities—even ones that had seemed like a good idea when I planned them.

I gained some very useful clarity about what energized me and what did not. I was building an interior foundation from which I could heal. Making these apparently simple adjustments helped me at all levels of being.

Venturing into Soul Territory

Mourning takes us deep into soul territory, which can be a daunting prospect if introspection is unfamiliar. Grief forces us to confront those troubling elements of self that involve the existential questions of identity, purpose and the very meaning of life.

We do not see the ways of the soul or the Divine. These two are uniquely joined in an agreement whose purpose is to transform our limited human comprehension into enlightened presence. When we suffer great loss, it is into the heart that our wise inner guide directs us.

No One Can Define Your Journey

Your spiritual heart is an inviolate place, full of comfort and the security of all that is good and true and beautiful about you. Here you may retreat in the dark hours of loss when all the familiar moorings of people, place and identity have evaporated.

Entering this holy place of refuge is vital because feeling safe in grief can be very challenging. Sadly, other people's opinions about how you should be conducting yourself may contribute to that sense of vulnerability. Yet, no one can plot or define how your journey through mourning will unfold.

Each of us must walk that rough road as only we can walk it—as only inner soul-communion can direct. Ultimately, we learn to hold ourselves in the loving-kindness with which our Wise Inner Counselor regards us.

Knowing that we are worthy of healing and capable of creating a new life is one of the most important concepts we can hold throughout our journey with grief. The child in us and our own children have much to teach us about allowing that new life to emerge.

Chapter Twenty-Three

LEARNING FROM THE CHILDREN

Christmas is often white here in Montana. Sadly, one year it was very dark for the children, parents and teachers at one of our local Montessori schools when their one-hundred-year-old barn burned to the ground.

Situated on several acres of land just outside of Bozeman, the school featured programs in the care of barnyard animals such as goats and chickens, along with some mice and a bevy of cats and kittens, all of which perished in the fire.

Shortly after that tragedy, the head of school, who knew about my grief education work, asked me to conduct a workshop with the upper elementary students to help them process their experiences.

Although many of the children had gone through other losses of pets and even some family members, this event had shocked their entire community. As it turned out, the children became teachers for all of us.

Beginning with a Story

I began the workshop with a little story taken from a musical play called *Peter and the Starcatcher*[24] which tells a story about Peter Pan's possible origins.

At a turning point in the play, Wendy is leaving Neverland. Peter is crying because they are best friends, and he does not want to her go away.

"It hurts," he says tearfully. She replies, "It's supposed to hurt. That's how you know it was important."

The children easily understood Peter's feelings. When I asked if that hurt could feel like a big hole in the heart, they agreed. They were eager to participate in an activity designed to help them fill in that hole.

The teachers had provided a large assortment of art and craft materials so each child could choose the medium they wanted to work in. I invited them to write something, draw or paint a picture or create a sculpture. Or perhaps they would like to compose a song or a dance to express their loss.

This part of the activity took about thirty minutes. As soon as the teachers and I noticed the students coming to a conclusion, we gave them an opportunity to select a partner and explain what they had created.

We timed this conversation so that each child had a few minutes to talk. Then I invited any of them who felt comfortable to share with the group what they had made and what they had experienced in telling a friend about it. When several of them did, I could see how they were comforting each other.

The Debrief

As I knew from my adult education workshops, the debrief at the end of an activity is at least as important as the activity itself. I walked the children through a visualization of what they had created and how their heart felt now. Then, anybody who wanted to share their experience with the group was welcome to do so.

Although their expressions varied, the hurt, the sorrow and the regret at not being able to say good-bye to their favorite animals became love.

When I asked, "What happened to your heart?" almost

without exception, the children said things like, "It got bigger. It got stronger." When I asked what the workshop had meant to them, they responded:

* "It made me appreciate mice more than I did."

* "It helped me realize how much I loved the animals."

* "It made me realize the joy I had felt before the fire was way more than the pain I feel now."

* "It helped me feel better about the fire itself."

* "It made me sadder for now."

The teachers were grateful to know about this comment from a very sensitive little girl so they could offer her additional attention and support. Without our debriefing, her ongoing grief might not have surfaced so quickly.

Children Helping Parents

A few days later, we held a community event in the evening so that parents could attend. Children from all age groups had selected songs to sing and several of the workshop students read their poems and told their stories.

Afterwards, we offered the parents an opportunity to express their own feelings about the loss. Several, with tears in their eyes and halting voices, told how their children had talked about the workshop and shared their own transformation with their parents. Their wise youngsters were helping their families deal with the loss that everyone was going through.

Children Process Differently Over Time

The teachers and I reminded the parents that grieving takes time. As children mature, they process their grief in different ways, depending on their age. Some regression can occur, so honoring the emotions that emerge later is very important.

As it happened, healing was an ongoing process embraced by the entire school community. Months after the workshop and community gathering, the head of school told me that adults and children continued to bring flowers to the site. Many families brought their own little memorials.

Even after a beautiful new barn was built as a home for new animals, many of the children referred back to the fire and the barn as a natural part of their ongoing healing.

The fact that they were still talking about their experiences was a very positive sign of both holding on and letting go.

Chapter Twenty-Four

No "Shoulds" in Letting Go

Nearly three years after Stephen died, his mother said to me, "I think I may be getting ready to let go of his ashes, but I'm not sure."

From her tone of voice, I wondered if she considered herself weak for not having scattered his ashes sooner. She sounded as if she were forcing herself to let go of something that would break her heart if she did.

"There are no 'shoulds' in letting go," I reminded her. "The sand in the hourglass will not run out before you decide that you're ready. If you want to keep Stephen's ashes forever, you can. Just because I released his remains last fall does not mean that you must. Don't do anything unless it feels right to you."

Following Inner Guidance

Before Stephen's cremation, I had a feeling that my grief journey and that of his family would not follow the same timetable. So I asked the funeral home to create two sets of cremains—one for me and one for his parents. It was one of my better decisions.

Another good decision was to give myself permission to mourn however I chose, in whatever manner arose within me, at whatever time grief should appear. Ever since we learned that Stephen's colon cancer was terminal, that practice had been my guiding principle.

Actually, this is how I have lived my life. For as long as I can remember, I have listened to my Wise Inner Counselor for direction, often taking dramatic action when something "felt right."

Following that unfailing guide led me to a path of spiritual discovery and soul growth that has been my life's saving grace. It also led me to Stephen and gave me the courage to marry him three weeks after our first date.

Throughout his illness and dying, inner guidance helped me release the life we had planned as well as presumptions about how each new phase of his final months would emerge. Eventually, the voice of Love eased me into letting go of the person I cherished more than life itself.

Internalizing His Essence

Almost immediately after Stephen's passing, I found it nearly impossible to accept that he was really gone. I was somewhere between thinking he should still be here and not being able to remember him at all.

So, I created a collage of photos of him—some from different stages of his adult life and some with the two of us together. It became my daily practice to place my attention on each image—rather like walking around the entire collage in my mind—until I could feel a portion of that image resting in my being.

I kept the collage on a wall in my dressing area for three years until I knew I had internalized the images and the core of who we were in the photos. That daily meditation helped anchor Stephen's presence in my heart and convinced me that we share an eternal essence—which gradually became more tangible to me than it had been when he was alive.

This ritual was one of the most transformative practices I adopted as part of my healing. I have recommended it to many people as a way to help them focus on the love that remains rather than trying to let go of the totality of the one who is gone. I have received emails from several people who said the process really helped them.

A Labor of Love

We know we are part of our loved ones and they of us. Yet as long as they are alive, we rely on their physical presence (or knowing that we can call or email them) to carry the essence of their soul. That is as it should be. However, once they are gone, a vital aspect of our healing process is to integrate that soul quality into our own hearts. That process takes time.

This is a labor of love that must develop naturally. It cannot be rushed. I think one reason we may not heal from loss is that we focus too much on trying to accept the absence of our loved ones rather than working to assimilate their soul qualities that were most dear to us.

Of course, this does not mean that we create shrines to our loved ones that keep us tied to the past so that neither we nor they can move on in our respective soul development.

There came a point when I realized that my collage was all about the past and that it had served its purpose. I had done the internalization work. I now contained those images. I tucked them into a scrapbook where they would be safe, but out of sight. I no longer needed to look at them. I knew that Stephen had moved on. Now I was able to do the same.

Timing Is Everything

There may be a detectable, even predictable, path to healing from great loss. However, only the present moment can reveal where we are on that path. Timing is everything.

Eventually, Stephen's mother began to feel that continuing

to keep his ashes was a burden to her and even to him. She told me she was feeling that he needed to be free. In a way, his ashes were letting go of her.

Shortly after our conversation, Stephen's parents and his younger brother hiked up a mountain path to a place overlooking a beautiful lake that was similar to the view from the Maroon Bells Wilderness Area where I had taken my portion of cremains the previous autumn.

Later, his mother told me that as they let go of the final portion of ashes, she felt a remarkable lightness, a sense of release and a deep knowing that waiting had been right and that letting go now was also right. A year earlier I had felt the same.

What impresses me about our individual experiences is how delicate and precise is the timing for these outward expressions of grief. And how gentle we must be with our own process of fully experiencing important elements of our bereavement before we try to let go of them.

As a dear friend whose mother recently passed away said to me one evening at dinner, "If you don't let yourself feel the grief, you also block the joy."

I agree.

Chapter Twenty-Five

OUR GREATEST ACT OF KINDNESS?

We usually think of loss and grief as being forced upon us by external circumstances. Sometimes—for the good of all concerned—we must initiate the separation ourselves. Leaving may be our greatest gift to those we love because of what our departure may teach us and them.

Leaving a Marriage

When I was twenty-six, I left my first marriage. Until that point in my life, this was the hardest thing I had ever done and I cried for weeks—partly over leaving my dog behind and partly out of guilt for abandoning my husband.

Yet, when I returned to our rental to pick up my belongings, I discovered that he had taken command of the household. The dog was brushed, the house was clean, the laundry was done and my brother-in-law (who was living with us) was shaved and wearing a new T-shirt.

Why had I been so worried? Yes, my "ex" tried to get me back and then became verbally abusive when I would not buy him a car. Still, he managed to adapt and make a new life for himself.

That event taught me a big lesson about taking the leap when inner guidance sends you a strong message to leave.

When Love Left Me

Circumstances were reversed when Stephen died. Losing the

love of my life was the worst thing that had ever happened to me. I know that leaving me behind was one of his greatest burdens in dying.

Stephen and I had never worked together, so he had not witnessed me being as self-reliant as I could be. He had not observed me in my frequent workplace role of project manager until our house was hit by lightning a few months before he died.

Because he was so sick, I had to manage communication and logistics with the disaster recovery company—a task I did so well that the project coordinator offered me a job. The events of those few weeks may have convinced Stephen that I would be okay if he passed on—which he did three months later.

Stephen's Greatest Act of Kindness

My sweetheart has been gone now for over thirteen years. I can unequivocally say that I have grown more as a person in that time than during any other period of my life. Losing Stephen has become the most *important* thing that ever happened to me.

His absence and my need for new purpose forced me deep into my inner psychological and spiritual resources as no previous life experience had ever done. I had to grow up emotionally and take responsibility for my home, my finances and my career decisions without my husband's physical support and guidance.

I also felt myself beginning to internalize some of the important spiritual principles that Stephen had been trying to help me understand throughout our eighteen years of marriage.

Did he have to die for me to make so much progress? I resist the idea, though it is probably true. Leaving may have been Stephen's greatest act of kindness to me, even though it broke my heart and his.

The Broken Heart Matures

A heart that is broken open is a heart that matures as it learns to gently tend the wound that can eventually heal. As the heart heals, it gains the courage to follow its own leadings in a way it probably never did before.

Having the courage to follow my heart was certainly my prayer when I made the decision to move to Montana, leaving my elderly mother in assisted living in Colorado.

I had never planned to move as long as she was alive. But four years after Stephen's death it became clear that I could no longer continue in the home he and I had created together. What had once been a symbol of future security had begun to feel like too much of the past.

The house contained so much of us as a couple that I could not move forward in that environment as a single person. Every room felt like an embrace—which was lovely, until the past began to hug too tightly. I was starting to suffocate.

Helping an Elderly Mother

As I was struggling with my living situation, my ninety-three-year-old mother's declining health was causing her to cling to me in a way that was not good for either of us.

After taking a serious fall and having to move into assisted living, she became increasingly fearful and dependent on me. She would invariably develop some kind of health crisis right before I was scheduled to leave on a business trip, miraculously perking up once I made the decision to go anyway.

"You know she's playing you emotionally, don't you?" said her primary care nurse one day when I remarked that my mom seemed to do better when I was away.

That was true. When I returned home, I would be met

with a litany of her complaints while she was frequently complaint-free with the nurses.

Building Self-Reliance

One of my mother's worst fears was that she would be sent to a nursing home. So, her thinking went, if she did not tell the nurses that something was wrong, she would not be sent away from her studio apartment, which—while not ideal—was at least better than being shut away in a tiny hospital room.

She was certain I would do everything possible to avoid sending her to a care facility, so it made sense that she would consider herself safe to complain to me.

The reality of both situations became clear—My mother was probably going to live for quite a while longer in her current situation, and I could no longer live in mine. So, I sold my house in Colorado, bought a smaller one in Montana and completed the move by the end of January of the following year.

When I returned to Denver for a visit in February, I could see that my mom was emotionally stronger and more self-reliant than when I left. Of course, she missed me and wished I could just pop over to see her several times a week. Nevertheless, I could tell that she was proud of her ability to navigate her own situation.

She had developed affectionate relationships with her caregivers and she had become genuinely interested in how I was moving forward with my life.

She received skilled support from the assisted living staff and the palliative care professionals who visited her regularly—and they reinforced her independence in ways I could not. She was putting real effort into working on her own psychological and spiritual progress because I was not there to lean on.

I was grateful for these changes because my Wise Inner Counselor had been adamant that leaving was critical for my well-being. My moving also turned out to be exactly what my mother needed.

The psychological rewards for self-reliance are enormous, and we can only bestow them on ourselves—as we were both learning every day.

Attuning to Life's Phases

As I write this, I can see that what determines if we should leave a situation or stay is if this phase of our life is complete. I have the sense that if our time to depart has not arrived, nothing will release us. If our time is up, nothing will hold us back.

As with so many aspects of life and love and loss, attunement with our wise inner guide will light the way forward, in whatever direction we are meant to go.

Chapter Twenty-Six

LETTING GO FOR LOVE'S SAKE

Letting go of our loved ones is excruciating. The attachments are not only emotional and spiritual, they are physical. Our very cells have been knit together. When our loved one leaves, the parting feels surgical.

Perhaps the only thing that makes the separation bearable is knowing that the person is in a better place—which can be a really burdensome cliché when other people say it to us. We must come to that realization ourselves. This is one of the few blessings of a lingering illness—seeing that the body has worn out and accepting the soul's longing to be liberated from the physical shell that has become a virtual prison.

For our loved ones, the pain of staying eventually outpaces the sorrow of going—which is when we find ourselves saying to them, "I'll be okay. You can go on if you need to."

This is what Love does. It lets go of love for love's sake.

The Alchemy of Forgiveness

Often, more subtle and difficult to release are the lingering hurts or injustices for past wrongs (real or imagined) committed against us or by us. These are the "unforgivables" we hang on to, sometimes for years.

If we are to be freed in mind and spirit, as the dying are more dramatically freed of their bodies, these residual feelings need to be transmuted.

The atmosphere on the Other Side seems to be one of abundant forgiveness. If our dearly departed could, I am certain they would urge us to bury the hatchet, treat one another with kindness and forgive ourselves and others with the unconditional mercy they are surely experiencing on the Other Side.

Have you ever noticed how, when you resolve a challenging situation or mend your differences with a person you find difficult, the problem seems never to have existed? It is dissolved, even transformed, possibly resulting in friendship where once there was only enmity.

Holding on to hatred or anger requires a lot of energy. When we truly forgive another person, we let go of the negative image in which we have imprisoned him or her, and we ourselves are freed. Forgiveness releases the pent-up energy of negativity and transmutes it into positive power.

Forgiving Ourselves

The most difficult person to forgive is often our self. We may forgive others for great abuses, but we cannot seem to forgive ourselves for what may be minor indiscretions.

No one is humanly perfect. Yet somehow, we think that we should be. We may kick ourselves around the block for things we believe we should or should not have done, thought or said.

In this frame of mind, where others see our special gifts, we acknowledge only imperfections. We create an icon of our failings that is impervious to the ministrations of all but the most determined of angels.

If we are to move on after great loss, we must surrender our most passionately held erroneous beliefs and learn to forgive ourselves as the Divine has already done.

After my mother's passing, I found that I had to forgive

myself for not being a perfect caregiver for her. Fortunately, the transmutative power of grief has a way of dissolving the desire for human perfection.

Even so, my reaching a point of self-forgiveness has been a key factor in grief's ability to step aside and encourage me to focus on living with a joyful heart.

Confronting Our Fears and Regrets

Before Stephen died, we were able to confront many of our fears and regrets and let them go. By the time he slipped away, we were not hanging on to past hurts or grasping at future miracles. We were simply present for each other.

I believe the sense of completion we achieved is one of the main reasons he was able to beam into my world the exquisite joy he found in the next one.

Closure or Completion?

I have always avoided the phrase "getting to closure"—as if we could end our grief like closing the books on our year-end financial statements. Rather, I prefer the image of young children who watch the same movie over and over until they can sing all of the songs and recite all of the dialogue.

Then they may put the film aside because they have internalized it. Although the story lives on in them, they have reached a point of completion. Even for adults, storytelling can be an effective way of integrating the finest soul qualities of the person who has gone on.

A Faculty of Soul

An element of bereavement that surprises many people is how they are obsessed with telling stories about the one who has died. I am convinced this is a soul faculty that is meant to help us heal our grief.

The narrative we feel compelled to repeat may contain an important aspect of our loved one's True Self that our soul is urging us to assimilate for our healing and growth. The narrative may also be showing us an event or characteristic that needs our forgiveness.

Each time we tell the same story, we are meant to learn something new about the person, how they lived their life and what that can mean to us.

Telling and retelling a particular story can gradually fill in a particular chasm of loss that opened in our being. When that absence has been replaced with a tangible presence of resolution, our need for the story disappears on its own. Separation is healed and we feel complete.

A Storyteller's Caveat

If we are using storytelling as a way of healing our grief, we must ask ourselves—Does my story support growth and regeneration or is it solidifying old wounds and misunderstandings?

Stories that heal are stories that evolve, that evoke a deep truth. They enlighten the teller and offer fresh perspective to the listeners so that all may be elevated.

Stories that are told only to revolve the past, without the intention of learning from what came before, are worse than boring. They can be wounding. Each time a tale is told from a sense of injustice or self-pity, it winds a coil of energy that depresses the listeners as it binds the teller to a past that becomes increasingly difficult to heal.

Here is another aspect of grief's wisdom—Uplifting stories climb the spiral of partnership and add golden threads of illumination to the garment of light that our soul will need for its own journey out of this world.

Discerning the Difference

I am a storyteller at heart, which meant that I had to be very careful not to continue telling the same woeful tale of missing my husband because the process was so natural to me. I was especially mindful of not burdening my friends who graciously offered a listening ear.

From time to time, I did seek out a therapist. While listening carefully and with a compassionate heart, a good therapist will point out when our stories are revolving without moving us toward resolving or learning.

As long as each repetition generates a positive momentum, there can be elements of the story that bear repeating. We may not be able to discern the difference, but an astute therapist will. Thankfully, mine did.

Stories Do Evolve

Ultimately, the stories I have told in workshops, articles and books have brought me to a place of deep gratitude for life's transformative hardships and losses as well as for its obvious blessings.

Chapter Twenty-Seven

Till Death Us Do Part

When we get married "Till death us do part" is the vow we often make. Although we may gloss over that statement in the wedding ceremony, we do remain at least partially aware that one of us is likely to die before the other.

What almost no one seems to understand is that death's apparent separation is not an end—especially to those called to service beyond the grave. The Other Side of this life is a vast universe of limitless collaboration where love and inner wisdom move our souls along a river of shimmering potential.

Holding on to that concept can be a difficult task in the midst of walking through the challenges of daily life. While we are very much alive, we give little or no thought to the possibility that an ending might be looming over the horizon.

Going Different Directions

In some ways, Stephen and I were more separate when he was alive than we have become since his death. We loved each other passionately, though often we loved each other differently.

Fortunately, when we read together on Sundays, worked on remodeling our town house, went shopping for home furnishings or took road trips, we were a unit—complete in each other as two halves of a whole fitting snugly together. But in our daily work lives, we were often miles apart.

I was intensely focused on self-actualization—determined

PART

Diving i

Dark

to prove myself in a career as a professional development trainer. That meant spending hours reading business books and course literature to catch up with my colleagues who had been doing training and consulting for most of their adult lives.

I knew Stephen was proud of me. I also knew that he was disappointed by how seldom I could (or would) join him in the spiritual practices he was exploring.

"Why can't you meet me where I am?" he would ask. I tried and succeeded when we could just hang out. But most of the time, I was not where he was in consciousness.

Stephen had long ago satisfied his need for a professional career. He possessed many competencies in areas of finance that qualified him for positions of responsibility which he had held with distinction. He was very proficient at his current job in budgeting for a large urban school district, but that work was not his main concern. His spiritual path was his career.

Even before he got sick, he was moving beyond self-actualization into the refined environs of self-transcendence. I can see now that his soul was urging him toward his spiritual destiny.

Is Knowing a Blessing?

These days, I have a deeper appreciation for how Stephen must have been challenged to balance the spiritual and mundane aspects of his path. I know that learning he was going to die from cancer was a severe trial that he worked hard to understand. Still, I wonder if knowing that his remaining days on earth were fast slipping away was a blessing to his soul.

Each of us is limited in how long our earthly sojourn will continue, yet we do not act on that knowledge. Instead, we flap away our days and nights as if we had all the time in the world.

Stephen knew his time was short. So, he focused the full

force of his being on leaving th
full of light. He released all u
himself for his soul's liberation

Although he may not ha
also striving to attain enough s
port me from the Other Side.

During the last six mont
of him drawing within—in a
It is clear to me now that Ste
down his life for the liberation
of rebirth. He was securing o
worlds and sustaining our miss

Comprehending at Last

After more than thirteen years
with me in my heart, I am begi
about the journey we walked as

When I settle into that
ease across the golden thread
with my beloved. In these mc
reminded that I am not only f
This is our shared mission, ar
happen to be the one with pen

As long as I keep hold
spirit and let go of anything tha
communion, death cannot touc

We, whom joy has graciously touched,
will answer, "Yes!" when it beckons.

For we will have come to know joy
as Spirit's reward for stepping off
into the Unknown,
embracing life's great challenges.

Chapter Twenty-Eight

COURAGE, PRACTICE & PRESENCE

Following Stephen's death, I had the distinct feeling that I was diving into deep, dark waters. I would touch bottom, catch my breath and then plunge in again, hoping to discover an insight that would carry me forward.

I found that my willingness to dive into such a morass was an act of courage that flowed from the wise heart of my True Self. Inner guidance spurred me into the deep, but it was my outer human awareness that had to take the first plunge.

Love Is Waiting

Getting to the bottom of grief's dark waters took practice. At first, I managed only a brief dive before I came up gasping for air. Still, I knew I could not force an end to mourning. Grief came in waves that inner guidance urged me to engage as a vital aspect of my ongoing search for healing.

During the worst hours of my grieving, I likened the experience to untangling a kinked garden hose so the water rushed out in a torrent, leaving me completely spent. And yet, I began to notice a sort of spaciousness that sometimes accompanied the aftermath. When I paid attention to that openness, I would occasionally feel a soft blanket of love cradling me body and soul.

As I learned to trust that I was not going to expire from grief, these episodes of love and comfort appeared sooner and lasted longer. That is when I came to realize that love was waiting for me at the bottom of grief.

Each time I allowed a wave of grief to wash over me, the courage and presence of my True Self became more apparent to my outer mind. I became increasingly aware that my soul had access to a reservoir of wisdom that was being opened in the presence of my Wise Inner Counselor.

The Quickest Way Through

In contemplating what really is a spiritual mystery, my sense is that self-discovery emerges from the courageous communion of our souls and our Wise Inner Counselor, who sustains contact with the ineffable presence of absolute Love.

This link is delicate and can easily be spoiled or disrupted by fear. Yet with time and practice, we can build a momentum of spiritual attunement that clarifies our perception of what is real.

Those moments may be fleeting at first, but through perseverance we can increase them. Although loss and grief will likely visit us many times in our lives, now we understand that diving into grief's dark waters is the quickest way through.

Following the Trail of Our Tears

When we lose someone we loved body and soul, we miss their presence. When we follow the trail of our tears all the way into the depths of their absence, we discover that we are not only missing them. We are missing our self—our True Self—the profound authenticity that once was ours.

In that moment, we understand that life is a pilgrimage in search of our soul's lost garden of reality. The grief journey is nothing less than a voyage back to our own personal Eden. We are all on an odyssey of regeneration and resurrection.

Healing our grief means a return to the soul's home of light that we carry as memory, deep within our heart of hearts.

Opening Windows of Soul and Self

We are born of joy. The Wise Inner Counselor holds the vision and the presence of that joy as a way to magnetize our soul back to its original estate. The inner guide is intent on freeing us from burdens of karma and the weight of the world, which condemns the Divine in us without ceasing.

Even if nothing tragic were ever to befall us, we would still be engaged in divesting ourselves of all unreality. We would throw back the curtains and open the windows of soul and Self.

Regardless of circumstances, in the innermost parts of our being we are determined to let the sunshine in to light up the room and beam out the love in our hearts to light up a world.

In those moments, the soul is so alive that it rises to the heart and merges with the True Self. We have that potential— that obligation. This is what loss and grief are trying to teach us.

A Journey of "Unbecoming"

Our journey through life is really about "unbecoming" everything that is not our True Self. The reason we partner with grief is to allow the brittleness of our habitual patterns to be shattered. The not-self is what is broken so the soul can be liberated from an overlay of limited thought and behavior.

So, we keep moving. We honor the realities and acknowledge the unrealities that rise to the surface of our awareness to be dissolved in light and prayer. In a way, each aspect helps us deal with the other. The darkness may reveal the light more vividly. When we listen for the inner voice of Love, its dawning illumination gives us hope of a way forward through the night.

We Will Be Changed

Love encompasses a universe of possibilities that allow us to reframe calamities into opportunities for spiritual, emotional and psychological growth. This love carries us through life's catastrophes in the way that is most appropriate for us individually—so we may achieve the very personal transformation that loss offers.

In the process, we learn to live the dramatically altered life we would not have chosen. We come to realize that, one way or another, we will be changed.

Love challenges us to clarify—Changed from what to what? Will we unconsciously sink beneath the waves in darkness and despair, or will we consciously dive deep to discover reservoirs of strength and endurance that offer us an acceleration of mind and heart?

When I persevered, I found I could reach a state of being that was full of meaning, a new sense of confidence, even peace. Not skipping steps was the key. I had to allow each turn of grief's spiral of partnership to teach me, to challenge my assumptions about myself, about others, about life in general.

This is a hero's journey our souls long to take. In our heart of hearts, we know there are vital lessons to discover.

The Remedy Lives Within Each of Us

When we tip over to the Other Side, our sense of the challenges of physical life disappears into ineffable radiance. Yet before we cross that threshold, there is labor involved. Bereavement's pervasive atmosphere of separation and our fear that it will last forever are major obstacles.

Throughout the journey, Love is the remedy which we may have to take on faith. In the end, the love we have shared with our dear ones is eternal, and everlasting Love is what we are called to embody until our days are fulfilled.

Love is grief's unfailing companion. To fully know one, we must know the other. Achieving a sense of completion and wholeness is the promise Love makes to each person who may suffer loss. In this earthly life, that is everybody.

Love's Promise

Love remains when all is taken from you,
    even your identity as half of a pair
    that alters when one must leave
    and one must surrender to thriving.

Not hiding, but embracing the life
    that, for a time, insists on pulling you
    away from your heart's desire.

That proves how strong you are,
    resilient and able to let go
    your sense of separation,
    to learn that both of you are whole,
    each of you complete
    in the world where you abide.

Two wholes make a totality;
    not merely a gathering of pieces,
    but a new reality arising
    when you two become one
    and know yourselves in none other,
    as you speak with a voice that sounds
    of quiet melodies sung in sweet unison:

A single note that birthed you
    in the beginning when you
    embraced new earthly existence
    and set out on this adventure
    to prove that love lives on forever
    for those who yearn to believe 'tis so.[25]

Chapter Twenty-Nine

THE POINT OF LOSS

I have come to the conclusion that possessing a heart that can be broken open is one of life's incomparable gifts and that experiencing great loss is a vital rite of passage.

Until the ones we cherish above all others are taken from us, we may not consider the impermanent nature of life here on planet Earth. Until dramatic change affects us personally, we can live in an illusory bubble of belief in consistency and stability—even a certain eternality of physical existence.

"Only other people suffer calamity," we tell ourselves. And that is true. Until it isn't. Then we must face being broken open.

And that, I believe, is the point of loss.

Reaching into Refined Realms

While bringing us to our knees, profound loss can also elevate our sensitivity to other realms of existence that we may not have considered either possible or important.

The veil between worlds thins when a soul takes leave of this plane. If we are fortunate enough to witness that departure and wise enough to embrace what can be a shared experience, we may reach into realms of light that can bless and comfort us throughout all the remaining days of our life.

When we embark upon our own personal journey with loss, we begin to understand in the depths of our being that our soul has been given a glimpse of its own starry destiny. Even as our beloveds were translated out of this world, we feel the change in ourselves.

Why Do We Grieve?

When a loved one dies, we mourn our loss, not theirs. They are lost to us, but not to themselves. In fact, they may feel sublimely found in the arms of their God. So why do we grieve?

We grieve what is temporary. We heal by discovering what is eternal. And we find elements of the eternal in the fresh perspectives we bring up from the bottom of our grief.

Resolving the Sense of Separation

Our souls long for Home—for that state of being that is infused with the Divine Love that encompasses all and gives all, even as it takes from us all that is unreal. This love is the unifying power that seeks to resolve our sense of separation.

While death vividly reminds us that we often feel abandoned, in truth, we are the ones who left. Lingering under the surface of conscious awareness is our soul's recollection of its original departure from the Divine in eons long past. In loss and grief, that memory comes to the fore, driving us to find a remedy.

If we are open to the remedy which is Love, we will let the desperate, primal feeling of emptiness urge us to accept the spiritual wholeness that our departed loved ones long to send us from their new home on the Other Side.

Dying Daily

We need not wait for someone close to us to die to embark upon this journey of self-renewal. We can do what all great spiritual traditions teach—we can die daily to those limiting elements of self that keep us stuck in an ego-centric smallness of character.

Loss is really about learning. Grief involves giving our-selves fully to the succor of our souls. And joy can suddenly appear when we open our minds and hearts to the intimations of love and hope that may emanate from the invisible world.

If we allow loss to break us open to the eternal possibili-ties that live within us, when the end of life comes to us—as it must—our death can be a tipping over into the fullness of the spiritual light we have been gathering each day as illumination, compassion and courage.

Rainbow Light

One need not die to step across
the bridge between worlds,
though they who live
may struggle in the journey
back and forth.

If we only knew how thin the veil
when pure Love opens hearts to hearts,
we would rush with joy to enter in
to sweet moments of communion

which angels long to share with those
who suffer from a cold belief
in borders and stark boundaries
that simply are impossible
in the rainbow light that joins us.

Chapter Thirty

RECONNECTING IN IRELAND

When I was a child I used to claim that my soul was Irish. More than sensing a national identity, I was tuning into the Celtic spirit that lies at the core of who I am.

Long before I met the Lafferty side of my father's family and before I was able to visit the land of those Irish ancestors, I longed for the green fields, high cliffs and wild seas that eventually welcomed me home to reconnect with Stephen's spirit.

The veil between worlds is thin in Ireland. This birthplace of poets, saints and scholars is renowned for its ability to inspire the literary, the artistic, the poetical and the spiritual. The very stones seem to speak of ancient wisdom.

Each of my visits to this mystical isle has been a journey into the mysteries of life and death. The land, the sea and the sky sing to me of their perpetual conversation of primal antiquity, awakening a quality in my heart which, once aroused, I have never tucked away—not even when I returned from pilgrimage.

Fearlessness in the Face of Death

Perhaps because the Irish have dealt with so much death from famine, invasion, forced emigration and near-destruction of their language and culture, they have a familiarity with death and an uncommon willingness to talk about the end of life.

The Celtic spirit has never been entirely tamed—its flame never totally extinguished. Part of that sensibility is an acceptance of the presence of departed loved ones, which is as natural to the Celtic mind as the rising and setting of the sun.

From the perspective of Celtic spirituality, this continuity between the Unseen and the seen creates a great network of light—as Above, so below. Fear has no place here, only a strong encouragement to fulfill our reason for being on earth with all the love and determination we can muster. Then, when our time comes, death really will be just like stepping into another room.

Awakening the Muse

The precious gift which I brought back from my first pilgrimage to Ireland was the bonding of my soul to Stephen's. That connection and the revelations that flowed from it ignited my ability to finish my memoir about our experiences.

When another opportunity to visit the Emerald Isle presented itself, I did not hesitate. I eagerly joined a tour led by a famous poet who was the host and guide. We were a diverse group of philosophers, musicians, therapists, photographers, writers and poets who avidly delved into the thin places of County Clare in the West of Ireland.

Until I embarked on this adventure, I think I had forgotten just how important poetry was to Stephen and me—and to our ability to maintain a strong soul connection between worlds. I soon discovered that being in the company of so many creative people was inspiring to my own muse.

One day the invisible world cracked wide open and set me firmly on a path that eventually led to my becoming a novelist as well as a poet.

Accessing Ancient Memories

On the day in question, our group hiked up a twisting mountain path that led to a ruined stone chapel. The small structure was little more than two walls tucked into a forest of dark green ferns and thick hazel trees. It was a mystical setting that seemed to contain deep mysteries of the past. That proved to be true.

When our host began weaving a tale of the ancient druids who had gathered in groves such as this to teach and pray, the atmosphere began to shimmer with an otherworldly light. As he recounted the details of druidic origins in Ireland's misty past, I felt myself transported to another time when I knew I had been one of these mysterious people.

This experience kindled vivid memories of past lives that gave me a whole new understanding of the shattering losses and heartbreaking griefs which our twin flames had shared in ages long forgotten. From that moment on, poems flowed from me and my connection with Stephen's spirit intensified.

A clear knowing of my Celtic soul returned to me on that pilgrimage. Now I knew I was meant to be a writer—perhaps like a bard of old. Poetry was opening a vast portal to my soul's expression of the sacred tie between me and my beloved.

Another Treasure from Ireland

I also brought home a deeper appreciation for the writings of the late Irish poet, philosopher and spiritual sage John O'Donohue.[26]

In one of my favorite quotes he said, "Our loved ones mind us." By this he meant that those whom we have loved and lost are not so very far away. In fact, he said they keep a loving eye on us as we go about our lives. And they do what they can to send us help in times of need.

In view of my own connection with the invisible world and the stories others have told me about theirs, I understand O'Donohue's perspective, which flows from a tender tradition of deep spirituality. I do believe that, in certain cases after a loved one's passing, elements of their higher consciousness may continue to beam light and love to those souls with whom they have strong heart ties. And so, they "mind" them.

As we integrate the spiritual qualities of our loved ones into our own being, the more clearly we may continue to hear the wise counsel they would offer us from the Beyond. For it is in the spirit of each one's True Self that we are forever united.

Honoring Our Loved Ones' Legacy

What if we were to turn around John O'Donohue's poignant statement? Do we mind our loved ones after they are gone? Do we enter fully into the bond we shared—or into the heavenly light that now surrounds them?

Are we willing to let that light divest us of our attachment to a sense of loss and open our hearts to the healing power of Love that emanates from inner guidance?

Do we try to imagine what souls on the Other Side might want us to learn from their contributions to life? To build on the legacy they have bequeathed to us? To further their service so that each and every one of our souls is continuing to climb the spiral of our holy partnership?

Writing this, I can feel a universe of departed souls urging us not to lose the wisdom they attained in their lifetimes—often at great cost to themselves and others. Above all, they want us to feel the joyful sense of accomplishment they experienced as they gave their very best efforts to life.

Gathering in My Celtic Soul

Attempts are old and pervasive, trying
    to sever the Celts from themselves,
    their culture and their precious land,
    the music of their consciousness,
    the language of their heritage.

Perhaps that's why a rebel spirit
    lives on in hearts that would be free,
    that chafe at foreign occupation
    from thrones and powers near or far.

Éire's soul is in her land;
    she's fought for her identity
    against all odds and centuries
    more consciously than other races
    that have simply disappeared.

Place your feet on Irish soil
    and feel yourself being gathered in,
    as if your heart feels championed here
    by those determined to be seen;
    so that your own soul rises up
    to recognize itself at last.[27]

PART SEVEN

Rising from the Ashes of Endings

Even in poignant circumstance,
when Spirit comes to sit with us,
our eyes fill up with joyful tears.

We know in our souls
we are not bereft,
for joy has made
its presence known.

Chapter Thirty-One

GRIEF'S FIERY ALCHEMY

I have often thought of bereavement as a refiner's fire. Those alchemical flames burn away the lead of human limitation leaving behind the gold of divine possibility.

When we allow ourselves to be purged by the cleansing flames of loss and grief, we can be transformed into our True Self. A slight singe will not do. For the alchemy to be complete, we must allow our limited self to be fully consumed.

Grief beckons us to this fire walk. It calls us to venture all the way in, to mourn even subtle daily losses so we become accustomed to the heat that transmutes elements of our lesser self. Otherwise, when loss suddenly shakes our world, grief's call can feel more like a shove.

Most days we are too busy to notice the opportunities life offers us to venture into the land of grief—whose only purpose is to refine our consciousness. This pilgrimage is meant to be a daily voyage in communion with the Divine, but we often do not see it that way. We have not been taught the lessons that life's inevitable changes would have us learn.

Reaching into Creativity's Flames

Grief's fiery alchemy is found in the creativity that can spark us back to life after loss. Almost like the formation of a diamond from a lump of ancient coal, elements of self-discovery emerge from the creative pressure that forces out all that is less than the sacred purpose that is ours to achieve in this life.

Our soul longs for the etheric fire that will release it from the burden of its worn-out home. Our soul wants to be clean and unencumbered as it journeys into invisible realms whose vibrations are more refined than the earthly Earth where it has been living. Its goal is the heat of spiritual transformation that will accomplish the alchemy of change.

This is one reason why our spoken invocations are so vital. Whether through prayer, mantra, chant or song, the sacred energy released through words uttered aloud in praise or supplication accelerates the process of regeneration.

The souls of those who are approaching the end of their earthly sojourn ride the light stream of our prayers from this world to the next. Our own souls pray to be transformed by the holy fire of bereavement, not destroyed by it.

When we allow the incandescence of grief to transmute the dross in our being, that light carries us through the darkness of the Unknown into the sanctuary of our own heart. Just as Stephen discovered the presence of joy in heaven, the result of grief's fiery alchemy in us can be joy on earth.

A Reason to Embrace New Grief

If we consign grief to dark corners of the mind, it grows cold and moldy and loses its transformational power. It sticks to the soul like cobwebs and blocks the sun of renewal that would shine if we let it.

Fresh grief wants to move us into our personal regeneration. We may be startled by bereavement's surges of powerful emotions. Yet, it is this energy that fractures us open so the light of inner wisdom can emanate through, showing us ourselves in bright, revitalized ways.

When loss visits us again—as it undoubtedly will—former griefs may reappear so we can heal them. But unless we infuse old grief with vigor and belief in our ability to heal, it can shrink back underground where it may activate unconscious momentums of doubt, fear, depression (even suicide), disease and the real or imagined death of purpose.

The Soul Drive for Discovery and Meaning

As we open our hearts to forgiveness and peace, we may find ourselves developing a generous hospitality toward all of life's transitions.

Our soul wants us to endow those turning points with a dynamic energy that keeps us moving from one rite of passage to the next—especially when those passages involve the death of a cherished person, pet or circumstance.

Even in the most heartbreaking of situations, it is this soul drive for discovery and meaning that allows grief to complete its work and step aside in favor of joy.

Chapter Thirty-Two

BEYOND RESILIENCE

Bounce back! Oh, how we wish we could return to some semblance of normalcy after suffering great loss. We pray for resilience—an elasticity of being that allows us to "withstand shock without permanent deformation or rupture."[28]

But we are not rubber bands; we are creatures of Nature. And Nature is always transcending herself. We are created to do the same. We can never go back to the way things were. We are not meant to. We are destined to grow beyond our habitual manner of thinking, feeling and behaving.

Growth does not come without pain. We are tried in the alchemical fires of loss, never more to go back to a lesser state of consciousness. When we courageously step into mourning the worst events ever to befall us, we can rise from the ashes of those endings as reborn overcomers.

Claiming Life

For twin flames, transcendence has been the purpose of our souls for eons. Yet continuing to lose each other lifetime after lifetime is unspeakably painful. Each experience of loss hearkens back to our original separation.

Spouses really do become one flesh. For twin flames that bonding is particularly intense. Despite our personality differences, Stephen and I knew that our soul essence was the same, and his death ripped the very heart out of me.

My desire to follow him through the veil was nearly over-whelming, for he did not go alone. He took with him that portion of myself that had been knit into his being—cell to cell, heart to heart, soul to soul.

The person I was in relationship to Stephen also took flight from this world—leaving me behind, missing that piece of my self as well as the entirety of my beloved.

His absence was like a black hole, threatening to pull what was left of me into the abyss. What felt like a mere fragment of my identity had to fight to survive—to find a point of reality as an anchor. Each day my fractured heart was challenged to declare its intention to go on living—to claim life, no matter what desperate thoughts might say otherwise.

More Than Bouncing Back

As days flowed into weeks and months and years, I eventually realized how much of Stephen's own heart he had left with me. Finding our way to wholeness has been a process of growing two complete hearts—his in spirit and mine on earth.

This growth has been and continues to be so much more than bouncing back. Many times over, we have transcended who we were in order to become more of who we really are. This ongoing transformation is an enormous gift.

We are born stronger than what may befall us. Death has no power over us because we are made of the very substance of a sacred reality. Life reaches far beyond a former state. We are let-ting go into the heart of the Divine where transcendence simply *is*. Spirit and love and joy are alive in every cell, in our heart of hearts and in the flow of cycles that refuse stagnation.

Stasis is not the way of life.

Transcendence as a Twofold Process
Stoke the inner fires and do the radical thing.
I will be there in the water and the flame
as I have always, ever been.[29]

These lines were written during my second pilgrimage to Ireland. They welled up from my being as the voice of Love that was speaking to me of strong encouragement and admonition not to give up. As I read these lines now, I can feel them as the prophecy of grief's future departure and joy's astonishing leap out from my heart.

The Water
Endings, transitions, loss, grief—they all throw us into the volatile waters of emotion where we must learn to stay afloat, despite the currents that threaten to swamp us. Here is where I confronted my fears of being alone, abandoned—bereft of my identity and unsure of my future.

Once I learned to collaborate with grief, the water buoyed me up. Bit by bit, I learned to rest in emotion, to pay attention to the rhythm of the waves. Almost like giving birth, I learned to breathe into contraction's pain. I gained trust in my body's innate intelligence. And I listened for direction from the midwife—the Wise Inner Counselor who guided me through the process of delivering my new self into a world that was so different from what I had known before things changed.

Water's Many Voices
Traveling in Ireland taught me that grief's watery nature is more than powerful waves and the uncontrollable turbulence of mighty rushing rivers. When I paid attention, I found many still

waters in the serene lakes and ponds that welcomed an after-noon's peaceful meditation.

The calm waters of the River Shannon where it spreads out into Lough Derg, the vast estuary on the Atlantic at Kenmare, the smooth waves that kiss the broad sands of Ventry Beach all served to still my restless emotions as nothing else had done.

In my heart I found holy precincts containing an ocean of possibilities for healing that spoke to me of an internal peace that hides in motion.

The Flame

Gaining my sea legs sparked the alchemical fires of creativity. The thin places of Ireland that spoke to me through water's myriad voices summoned my innate will to live, to strive, to learn, to grow and eventually to seize the opportunity that arose from the destruction of life as I had known it.

Any creative act is also an act of courage. Manifesting something out of the nothing that endings leave in their wake requires trust in the process as well as confidence in our ability to stay the course.

We do not know what the end result will be. We are not meant to know. Our goal is to create a human "becoming"—a person who is forged in the phoenix fires of transformation. And who, once touched by this alchemical heat, will retain a strong affinity for self-transcendence.

Dancing in the Flames of Regeneration

According to legend, the phoenix rises majestically from the ashes of its own destruction. This fire bird must be completely consumed in the flames before it can be born anew. The embers must grow cold before a quickening spark can ignite in the ashes of the old form.

Here is a mystery the phoenix would have us learn—Only that which is impermanent and no longer useful is ultimately consumed in the refining fires. When we willingly dance in the flames, allowing our old self to be reduced to ash, we can rise again—purged and purified—ready to take on the next phase of our incarnation as a wiser, more vibrant version of our Self.

Life becomes richer, increasingly flavored with a sweetness that cannot be tasted except when the flames of transcendence have burned away many impediments to our soul's liberation.

In those moments, like the phoenix, we know for certain the future will not find us returning to life as it used to be.

Chapter Thirty-Three

Phoenix Rising

Phoenix fire is the sensation I feel sometimes when my Wise Inner Counselor sends me a particularly timely or surprising awareness. These inner realizations are like an ignition, a kindling—not merely an understanding, but also an impetus to become more of my True Self.

An image or idea will sail into my mind and travel to my heart. There it expands, intensifies and sets my heart to spinning and burning with a heat that eludes explanation, except to say, "In this moment, I am changed."

Here is gnosis—the instantaneous knowing that impels action, service, humility, prayer and surrender to a divine will. In those moments, I am called to sacrifice some paltry aspect of limited human reasoning that can be tossed into the refining fire of transformation's alchemy.

After Stephen was gone, I claimed the fire bird as the symbol of my own resurrection. I needed all the inspiration I could get. I certainly felt as if my world had been reduced to ashes. And yet, I had to keep moving.

The Need for Motion

Recently, some colleagues and I were discussing the importance of physical activity as a way to balance the many hours we spend at our computers. That need for movement is even more acute when we are dealing with the emotions of grief.

Following the death of a loved one, our time may be filled with myriad tasks of settling their estate, which require us to focus our attention away from our grief. This can present a major challenge because of how loss impacts clear thinking.

However, I have come to realize that the necessity of managing activities in the physical plane is one way that life and inner guidance prevent us from wallowing or going numb. Although we may long to simply disappear, severe withdrawal from the present moment can push grief into the unconscious where it wreaks havoc with our body, mind, heart, soul and spirit.

The Grace of Movement

As we navigate the choppy waters of bereavement, physical movement allows important lessons of inner wisdom to emerge gradually as we are able to assimilate them.

We need to sift through what was so we can discover what remains and what can grow. I definitely found this to be true in the first four months after Stephen's passing. In the midst of crying rivers of tears, I stayed very busy.

Although we had organized most aspects of our joint estate, there were certain legal matters that could only be finalized after the death. In addition, I was planning Stephen's memorial service with live music and eulogies from family and friends.

I was also remodeling the entire second floor of my town house—a project which Stephen and I had agreed I would do after he was gone.

At the same time, I finished writing the first draft of my memoir, which remodeling actually helped me accomplish. The physical activity allowed my mind and emotions to rest while my hands and body kept moving.

Fresh perceptions of what I was writing often came to

me as I was cleaning fixtures, painting walls and staining what seemed like miles of dark trim.

Plunging to the Bottom—Again

Of course, too much of a good thing is still too much. In a way, I became a poster child for what is called bereavement burnout. Eventually, my body cried, "Halt!"

One Sunday morning I woke up unable to move. That day I came to the unwelcome conclusion that I must find a new home for Bentley—my precious black standard poodle who had grown into too much dog for me.

Once more, I plunged all the way to the bottom of a broken heart. And I gained a deeper understanding of what the fire bird experiences when it is consumed in fires of its own exuberance.

The phoenix really does die. It must allow itself to be completely dissolved by the purifying flames. I am not sure it ever truly knows if it will rise again. If the fire bird knew in advance that it would be reborn, the whole process would be a fraud.

But it is not. The expiration is for real. That moment when a new fire kindles and the phoenix bursts forth is as astonishing to the bird as it is to those who witness its rising.

Cherishing the Flames

Somewhere in my physical collapse, I also discovered that in order to emerge from bereavement burnout I had to allow my pride to be consumed. I reached a point of humility and surrender that finally allowed Spirit to help me. Until then, I had been holding too tightly to the projects I had taken on until I could go no further.

I do not recommend complete physical exhaustion as a personal growth strategy. However, I do recommend allowing the process of abject grieving to carry us to that place of total vulnerability where we stop trying with all of our human might to control the circumstances of our life and sorrow.

At the absolute bottom, when we feel completely lost, the great cosmic burner ignites and a new phoenix begins to emerge from the bitter ashes of hopelessness and defeat.

I still have my busy days. Sometimes they are unavoidable, although now I am more adept at recognizing when my mind starts spinning. Then I let myself rest in the generative soul fires that are my point of serenity.

I cherish the opportunity to burn in the creative flames that send my heart soaring. In those moments, my soul is a happy bird—a reborn creature, clothed in the brilliantly hued plumage of a resurrected phoenix.

Stephen's Phoenix Moment

This principle applies in etheric realms as well as in the physical and the mythic. When I meditate on the first hours of Stephen's soul transitioning out of his body, what comes to me is a moment of genuine surprise and delight that he was surrounded in joy as well as the light and love he had anticipated.

I can see him hurrying to tell me that he had risen into an ecstatic state and that, at least for a few hours, he was allowed to fold that cloak of bliss around me. He literally pulled me into his heart as the two of us soared like a pair of radiant fire birds.

Stephen honestly had not expected to receive such a glorious translation from earth to heaven. That is what makes this whole phoenix metaphor so powerful.

As with many myths, this story is likely based on reality. I wonder—Does the soul appear like a phoenix as it lifts off to its new home in the sky? I would not be surprised.

Chapter Thirty-Four

EXPRESSING OUR TRUE SELF

E very soul is beautiful. When grief urges us to open our hearts, it is putting us in touch with an internal repository of beauty we may never have known or admitted that we contain. Offering our unique beauty to the world may be our highest service to life.

Each time we use our imagination to tap into that wellspring of inner genius, we are weaving luminous threads into the garment of light that will one day clothe our soul for its final journey Home.

How we go about enhancing our corner of the world is how we are expressing our innate creativity. Think about what you do so naturally that you take it for granted until someone points out your talent. Whatever your special abilities, that is how you are beautiful and creative.

The Key to Creativity

Inspiration's call to creativity will reveal our natural talents. Even in my darkest days, when I remembered to listen for how my soul wanted to express itself in poetry or prose, grief receded into the background.

The key to creativity is that you cannot make it happen. What you can do is establish an environment that invites fresh ideas. My muse naturally emerges when I quiet my busy mind and listen for inner guidance.

Clearing the Way for Connection

After Stephen was gone, the fact that I had a book to write was my lifeline. Transcribing the hundreds of pages I had journaled about our life together plugged me into my native creativity as a storyteller.

The hours I initially spent reviewing my notes about our journey of love and loss began kindling my soul's connection with Stephen's soul on the Other Side. This awakening cleared the way for the electrifying connection we made in Ireland.

The Gift of Your Soul Poetics

Your soul is eager for you to experience your own electrifying connection with the highest expression of who you really are. If you have been visited with heartbreaking loss, the gift that awaits your discovery at the bottom of grief's dark well could be the exquisite realization of your soul's inner beauty.

The extraordinary uniqueness that only you can offer to life is what I call your Soul Poetics.[30]

I first came upon the term "poetics" in John O'Donohue's work. The root of the word means "to create." Simply put, the poetics of our soul is how we express what is most beautiful, noble and real about us. The great life question is this—Will we have the courage to offer that creation to the world?

Imagine a shy child who longs to give her gifts to those she adores and yet is wary of being rejected or misunderstood. Many of us are like that. We may spend ages looking for a way to unlock the mystery of our deep soul talents in a manner that will not scare us.

Unfortunately, as long as we tiptoe around the edges of life or distract ourselves from our true calling by following other people's dreams or mandates, we will never realize that fear of disclosure is the least of our worries.

Our soul's real concern is that time is fleeting. Opportunity to forge the path we were born to walk may not knock more than once or twice. We may intuit that an adjustment in our priorities is needed, but that could mean changing what we do and who we think we are—a prospect we may vigorously resist.

Loss Shifts Our Priorities

If we are fortunate, loss will come along and turn our world upside down. Suddenly, the externals we feared to lose have little meaning. Wealth, status, possessions, the extent of our social media presence—society's materialistic measures of worth fall away in an instant.

Our outer self is suddenly bereft, unmoored from all that is familiar. We are at the mercy of the Unknown. And yet, in the midst of chaos and confusion, a way forward starts to dawn.

We begin to evaluate what remains.

We may have lost our home, yet our family is safe. Our dearest beloved may have died, yet we still have a shared mission to complete. We may have lost our sense of identity, yet time remains for us to discover the Self we have kept hidden behind obligations that are unworthy of who we really are.

Loss cracks us open so the light of our inner divinity can shine through. Grief shows us the way through the darkness. Joy waits just around the corner to illumine the life we did not have the courage to claim—and now we do. Nothing else matters except finding our way to the truth of our being.

Unlocking the Soul's Full Measure

When we allow loss of the familiar to help us discover opportunities within the Unknown, our ability to creatively solve life's problems can blossom like a garden in spring.

I read somewhere that we are as powerful as our willingness to perceive, receive and apply our abilities—whatever they may be. This is why no one can predict or determine your journey from loss through grief to joy. The poetics of your soul's full measure is the treasure you have had in your pocket all along.

Beauty
written in the lush green fields of Ireland

Beauty floats on the breeze
Of Spirit's presence.
She flies up on angel wings
Spreading dew drops of perfection
To quicken the hearts of all
Who will receive her gifts with gladness.

She bonds her place and all who live
With stories of the past,
Giving courage for today
And blessings for tomorrow.

The telling is her treasure.
Ears feel Beauty as her voice
Tickles their inward parts,
As bodies rest easy in the green grass
Where Beauty's delicate bare feet
Have cleared a path
And faeries hold up firefly lanterns
To light the way.

Chapter Thirty-Five

EMBRACING CREATIVITY'S SPIRIT

For quite some time after Stephen's passing, his mother and I shared profound conversations about our experience of losing this precious soul who had been a shining light in his family.

There were aspects of Stephen's approach to his dying that he had not explained to his parents or his two brothers and which his mother, in particular, wanted to understand. I was always glad for these opportunities to tell her stories about my love for her son.

Going Creative in Grief

Stephen's mother was a textile artist. When I first met her, she was working on a full-sized loom in her sunny studio where she created some exquisite wall hangings along with blankets for new babies and other gifts for family members.

Eventually, our conversations centered less on Stephen's absence and more on our being creative people, which we felt helped to facilitate our healing. We agreed that already being engaged in a creative practice gave us a window into the often otherworldly and amorphous nature of mourning that troubles many people.

Our loss was not any less painful because we could turn to weaving or writing. Rather, our familiarity with the empty loom, the blank page, the fresh inspiration of a yet-unformed project gave us a unique perspective into how grief can work in the apparent void of the Unknown. We trusted our creative process to transform us into more genuine versions of ourselves.

Being Done with Death

Then my own mother died and my ability to create my way through loss abandoned me. The only thing I knew to do was to stay in motion until some semblance of reality could dawn in my outer awareness.

My mother was well into her nineties and her health had been declining for a number of years. We had already put her affairs in order, so there were few details of her estate for me to finalize after her passing.

However, I found myself swirling in confusing psychological elements of our relationship that I could not seem to resolve, even with a counselor's help. Although I had been teaching workshops on processing grief, the pain and suffering of my mother's last weeks overwhelmed me.

I had not changed my mind about how the end of life could be. I just could not deal with another one. If anyone asked, I said I was done with death.

Once More in Motion

So I traveled. During the next eighteen months I went on fourteen trips. Some by car. Others by air. Most were domestic and at least one took me out of the country.

I visited people I had not seen in years. I frequented the theatre and attended personal-growth workshops. I did everything except write. Not even my muse had words for whatever was trying to be born within my psyche.

I had no interest in death or grief or dramatic change. Since those were the only topics I had been writing about, I stopped—completely—until a wise friend happened to mention that April was "Write-a-Poem-a-Day-Month" and my internal logjam broke.

Giving My Soul a New Voice

After months of travel, I returned to my journal and started writing poems. Hundreds of lines of verse began flowing from the very depths of my soul.

These were not poems of grief. They were vibrant expressions of new life being born in me. I felt as if my soul were crying out to be liberated from the shroud of mourning. I was going deep into my psychology and spirituality while giving my imagination free reign.

I published many of those poems later that year, although that had not been my original intention. At the time, I was simply unleashing the phoenix-fire of creativity that was burning away layers of old, worn-out aspects of my being that had not been able to move forward into the future that was calling me.

I was also connecting with Stephen's spirit in new and powerfully tangible ways. The future remained obscure, but I could feel it pulling me to a bright new tomorrow. I entered into a dynamically creative process that emanated from a soul reality I had never experienced in quite the same way.

There was an honesty to these early verses that encouraged me to keep going. Once I gained a momentum in that daily conversation with hidden parts of my Self, I began to find my voice—not only as a writer, but also as a human being.

Chapter Thirty-Six

CREATIVE LIFE, SPIRITUAL LIFE

I have heard it said that if you have a creative life you also have a spiritual one. That is certainly true for me. The communion that Stephen and I share has proved to be highly creative as well as profoundly spiritual.

Immersing myself in my journal, in the twilight hours of dawn and dusk or late at night when the earth around me is still, my soul feels called to reveal itself as it does at no other time.

I relish these hours as the most rewarding of my life. Here in sublime silence is where my True Self speaks to me of liminal places as it tells me stories of life and love that I once knew and had forgotten.

Becoming the Mystery

After I fulfilled the vision that I was meant to survive Stephen and write our story, ideas for more books continued to emerge. As each book has revealed itself, writing from the depth of our communion between worlds has taken me further and further into a profound understanding of our twin souls.

The only way I have been able to write each new book has been to drink the full cup of inspiration which presents itself at the time—to imbibe the mystery, to live the mystery, to become the mystery.

In that light, I would like to tell you the story of how I became a spiritual romance novelist—a *seanchaí* (pronounced shanakee), as the Irish call their storytellers—and how my first novel, *The Weaving*, has direct bearing on the path Stephen and I walk as twin flames.

Many Lives, Many Roles

Every poem, every chapter, every story in my books has originated in my journals as the unfiltered musings of my heart, mind, spirit and soul.

While I am immersed in writing fiction, I do not think of my characters as containing facets of my own being or people I have met, yet I know they do. My career in musical theatre certainly supplied me with intriguing examples to draw from—both on and off stage.

One need not be an actor to sense that we have lived many lives and played many roles. From pauper to prince, conquered or conquerer, villainess or heroine—our souls retain the records of all our embodiments.

Should we venture into the narrative of those lifetimes, we contain psychological archetypes at deep levels of being that can fill out the cast of any drama we might wish to convey of our soul's evolution through time.

In a way, our story belongs to everyone. In the case of *The Weaving*, the main characters represent many twin flames. They would not let me alone until I told their story—which had begun in a different book many months before I realized that I had first met them as druids in a ruined chapel in Ireland.

Tales from the Etheric

Trusting my imagination to create locations and characters began in earnest with my third collection of poetry, *Idylls from the Garden of Spiritual Delights & Healing.*

These verses take the reader on a magical journey through an etheric garden that sometimes appears in NDEs or in past-life regression hypnosis. Although I have experienced neither of those thresholds between the spiritual and the material, my muse sprang into action when I decided to imagine being in that garden. Soon I was writing about gnomes, fairies, spirit beings and fantastical animals who all had tales to tell.

Discovering Myself as a *Seanchai*

Idylls is really where the whole storyteller adventure began. I have since discovered that these verses are a visionary sojourn that the druidess Alana experiences with her twin flame, Ah-Lahn. He is a master druid who has crossed over to the Other Side, where she meets him while she is in a dream state.

Toward the end of the book, Ah-Lahn tells Alana that she must return to her own world because he wants her to tell their story. At the time, I had no idea what that could mean and did not pursue it. However, inspired by *Idylls*, I continued writing poems without knowing where they might fit. What I did know was that these verses were very intent on being committed to paper.

Meanwhile, I also wrote a couple of chapters about Alana. And then one night, an epic story of the druidess and her twin flame began to unfold in my imagination. I soon realized, "This is a novel! I have to become a spiritual romance novelist!"

Mysteries Within Mysteries

Almost immediately the story completely took over my life. I was not only writing dialogue and descriptions, I was in the scenes. Often, I would find myself watching them play out in my mind like a movie.

Anyone observing the process would have seen me typing as fast as I could to capture the scenes while the ancient druids Alana and Ah-Lahn revealed mysteries within mysteries.

The book that emerged as *The Weaving* is the story of twin flames through a series of embodiments. It shows how, lifetime after lifetime, they have gone through the same lessons, the same challenges, the same opportunities—often confronting the same adversaries.

The book begins and ends with the druids' current incarnation as Sarah and Kevin, a couple who are having relationship problems. Although the story comes to a harmonious conclusion, this adventure was not over. Not only was it not over for Sarah and Kevin, it also was not over for other pairs of twin flames that we meet in *The Weaving* as druids, bards and healers.

These couples each had their own stories to tell. They had also reembodied in modern times and were dealing with the consequences of their own past lives, past initiations and past challenges which they had not resolved.

With those stories begging to be told, I published the *Twin Flames of Éire Trilogy* to further explore the question—What does it mean to reunite with the twin of your soul?

Living the Mystery

These days I have a sense that my becoming a mystical writer and storyteller is a path of self-discovery which I have pursued for a very long time. Allowing my creativity to fully flower has given me incredible insights into the challenges our twin flames and others have encountered throughout the ages.

It is clear to me now that I was activating memories from past lives as I entered into these stories. I was accessing a presence of etheric realms that I had never dared to embrace, and every new insight brought me closer to Stephen.

I know my relationship with my beloved is richer, more understanding and more forgiving because of *The Weaving* and the trilogy novels which followed. The proximity that Stephen and I experience now is a direct result of the deepening insights I gained while writing about these other twin flames.

Co-creating with the Divine

I am not exaggerating when I say that the creative process has saved my life and resurrected my soul. Writing sustains my connection with Stephen and with my God.

I am convinced that creativity is a vital key to healing our souls. When we summon the courage to step into the Unknown, we may find ourselves putting together the puzzle of our real identity. Whatever our individual talents, creativity is what can reassemble all the disparate facets of our being into the totality of our True Self.

We become co-creators with the Divine—one of the most significant blessings the journey from loss through grief to joy has to impart to us.

Chapter Thirty-Seven

AIMING FOR THE STARS

After finishing *The Weaving*, I decided to collect some of the poetry that had appeared in the novel.

As I settled into the deep soul expression of these poems, I slipped into a profound meditation with Stephen. I began to hear and feel him with a clarity I had never experienced. New poems were spilling onto the pages of my journal and many of them were in Stephen's voice. There was a particular quality of cadence and rhyme in these poems that was different from my own verses. I knew they were from my soul's twin.

Nearly every night for a month, as I sat alone in the silence of my room, new poems arrived. Many were about the soul's spiritual yearning and the longing of twin flames for reunion. Others described images of Stephen's experiences on the Other Side. Quite a few were conversations between our two souls. Several poems were from the Spirit of Love.

As I entered into deep communion with my beloved, my heart burned with a creative eros. Every poem became like an orb of ineffable love. Even now, as I write this, my heart expands. I am enfolded in the vibration of a sacred inner place of sublime creativity.

Our Love Reaches Out

In this sanctuary of the heart, the love of our twin flames lives in us and reaches out to the world. Here also is the place of grief's departure, to which it has never returned with its previous intensity.

I still weep at sad books or movies. Beautiful music can move me to tears. I am deeply touched by other people's losses, and I acutely resonate with the pain they are experiencing in their own journey through grief's dark waters.

However, the abject, howling, primal mourning that rushed through me when Stephen died has been replaced by an indescribable love. That love transports me to a celestial realm of wholeness where our hearts and souls are no longer separate. Here we are one in the fullness of joy.

The Need for Transmutation

Touching into this space is immensely humbling because it comes with great responsibility. Maintaining the integrity of our connection takes effort. Ongoing resolution of negative elements in my personal psychology is imperative.

Triggered by loss, accelerated by grief and fulfilled by joy, profound transmutation is the alchemy which our Wise Inner Counselor has urged us to embrace from the beginning of this and many lifetimes.

Transmutation is vital for any soul who desires to achieve liberation from the rounds of rebirth. For twin flames who are called to a mission beyond the veil, this work is essential. The process of unification transforms our perception of being two separate souls into a wholeness that is far greater than the sum of our parts.

Minding Each Other

Stephen and I know we have been given into each other's care. Our mutual acceleration on the path of self-discovery is our primary concern so we may continue to be of service to others.

We know that the future of our mission depends on how well we "mind" each other, as John O'Donohue says. When we place our full attention on the love between us, a vibrant sense of our best Self flourishes.

Like weavers of old, we are creating a tapestry of new life with golden threads that shimmer in the light of joy's gifts as they radiate from our hearts in this world and the next.

Absence simply cannot exist in the same plane with the fullness of love which is our true reality. That is what loss and the natural, necessary process of grieving are meant to teach us.

Our Mighty Network of Light

Planet Earth is in desperate need of a light infusion. As we rise from the ashes of endings, the creative luminosity we bring to that process is for the healing of others, as well as ourselves. We support souls on both sides of the veil between worlds.

Each of us has a mission that extends beyond death. The newly deceased need our prayers to reach the heavenly realms to which their souls aspire. We who remain may further important causes we shared with those who have preceded us in the homeward trek.

Together, we form a mighty antahkarana—a network of spiritual light and presence. We are dedicated to purposes that have occupied the attention of saints, sages, poets and philosophers for millennia, and for which we and our soul families may have given our last breath in countless ages of the past.

Until our time comes to depart this earth, we lay down our lives for each other in large ways and small so that all may continue to learn and grow—before and after death.

Here is love by love for the sake of love. All for the purpose of Love—which has always been to extend itself to life. When we determine to give our lives for our sisters and brothers, the love that brought us to this place can liberate a world in need.

Setting Stephen's Course for the Stars

One day in the last year of Stephen's life, before he became visibly diminished by the cancer that was stealing his vitality, I asked him if there was anything he wished he could have done.

"I don't have a bucket list," he answered thoughtfully.

I could see how that was true. He had lived fully and deeply. He had so completely surrendered to the will of God, all he desired was to be subsumed into that will.

Several months before we had this conversation, the one thing he *had* wanted to do was to rent a Mustang convertible and drive with the top down high into the Rocky Mountains for a weekend retreat. After that, Stephen set his course for the stars and never looked back.

A State of Transcendent Being

Shortly before he stopped working he declared—almost as if he were answering a question I had not asked—"Eventually, the soul's only prayer is praise."

He said he had ceased to focus his meditation on anything other than a worshipful union in which no separation could exist between him and the Divine that he could feel alive in his heart.

"When I meditate, I know who I am," he said as he tried to explain to me the sensation of his soul reaching up to the stars and in to his divinity.

This is the transcendent state of being that I can feel him urging all of us to attain. More than anything, he wants us to realize the full potential of our True Self—and to share in all he is experiencing in that edenic realm of never-ending creativity and universal service that he now calls Home.

Stephen expresses his heart's desire in the following poem, which was written in a moment of our profound communion between worlds. When I read these lines, I feel myself transported once more to that glorious day when he first declared, "There is joy in heaven!"

Now, I invite you to travel with my sweetheart as he soars through the realms of light and love and joy which he so earnestly longs to share with every one of us.

Galaxies

Whirling, spinning, spiraling,
bursting, scintillating,
projecting starry clusters
into deepest space.

These I have seen!
O, that I could bring you with me!

Rise with me that we might fly
beyond worlds,
to star systems
hurtling through space,
yet poised in perfect stillness,
focusing all their will
upon the fiery center
at the nucleus of all creation.

I am with you,
even as I am everywhere in cosmos.

Feel my passion burn in you
as soul recognizes soul once again
and reunion takes on
new flavors of ecstasy.

Where you are, there am I also,
hidden in the deepest wellspring
of your holiness,
the inner galaxy whose starscape
you have only begun to explore.

Worlds await your presence.
Let my love carry you there,
for we have labors yet undone
and visions of grandeur to fulfill.

Mystics gather, indeed,
in joyful anticipation
of words not yet spoken,
communion soon to be felt
and joy unbounded,
quivering in gratitude
for its imminent release,
as untold treasures of experience
are just ahead.

Let not your mind be anxious;
the path that leads
beyond the summit is not dark.

It bursts like fireworks
through veils of separation
into soul unities

where all is oneness—
essence to essence, galaxy to galaxy,
dancing for eternity
in the great T'ai Chi
of life becoming Life.

Step through the veil with me,
and come to know the glory
of your being and mine.

We are truly one
in the Love that is Reality.

I am the glow in your breast,
the warmth of tears that spring
in answer to my presence.

Swing wide the doors of consciousness
and see me standing before you;
feel me present with you
where I have always been.

Ten thousand light-years are nothing
to the fullness of my love.[31]

Joy is present when souls are born.
And at the end of their days,
it leads them Home,
thinning the veil
for those who would see—
offering a glimpse of life's bookends
that it waits upon so faithfully.

ACKNOWLEDGEMENTS

To my fellow travelers who have been stalwart companions on this book's journey from concept to completion, may you be blessed beyond measure.

To my colleagues, Theresa McNicholas, James Bennett and Janice Haugen, may you know the depth of my gratitude for all that you do and all that you are.

To my darling Stephen and our generous teachers, may the work of my hands and the meditations of my heart be proof of your faith in me, all the way to the stars.

To you, dear reader, may your soul be eternally cradled in a shimmering sphere of ineffable love.

Notes

1 Cheryl Lafferty Eckl, *A Beautiful Joy: Reunion with the Beloved through Transfiguring Love* (Livingston, MT: Flying Crane Press, 2019) p. 65-67.

2 For more information about the Wise Inner Counselor, see Eckl, *Reflections on Being Your True Self* and *Reflections on Doing Your Great Work*.

3 Eckl, *Bridge to the Otherworld* (Livingston, MT: Flying Crane Press, 2016) p. 3-4.

4 Every event that has occurred on earth has been recorded in the spiritual substance known as akasha. Those records remain where the events took place unless and until they are transmuted by the sustained invocation of spiritual light.

5 Such instances could be considered a type of clairaudience—defined by. *Merriam-Webster's Collegiate Dictionary, Eleventh Edition* (Springfield, MA, 2004) as the power or faculty of hearing something not present to the ear but regarded as having objective reality.

6 Helen Greaves, *Testimony of Light: An Extraordinary Message of Life After Death* (New York: Jeremy P. Tarcher/Penguin, 1969, 1999). This is the fascinating account of life beyond the grave that was communicated telepathically to Helen by her longtime friend Frances Banks after her passing. Frances gives detailed descriptions of her life and service to souls beyond the veil.

7 Eckl, *Poetics of Soul & Fire* (Livingston, MT: Flying Crane Press, 2015) p. 64-65.

8 See the Solas Bhríde Centre and Hermitages https://solasbhride.ie/

9 Cynthia Bourgeault, *Love Is Stronger Than Death: The Mystical Union of Two Souls* (New York: Bell Tower/Random House, Inc., 1997, 1999).

10 Mystical traditions call this process by a variety of terms: weaving the wedding garment, creating the deathless solar body, putting on the body of Christ. I believe each describes the result of profound spiritual practice.

11 Eckl, *A Beautiful Joy*, p. 13.

12 Ibid., p. 77.

13 Eckl, *A Beautiful Death: Keeping the Promise of Love* (Livingston, MT: Flying Crane Press, 2010, 2015, 2022).

14 Eckl, *Poetics of Soul & Fire*, p. 105-107.

15 John Welwood, *Toward a Psychology of Awakening: Buddhism, Psychotherapy, and the Path of Personal and Spiritual Transformation* (Boston: Shambhala Publications, Inc., 2002) p. 11-14, 207-13.

16 Eckl, *A Beautiful Death*, p. 152-153.

17 His Holiness the Dalai Lama, Archbishop Desmond Tutu with Douglas Abrams, *The Book of Joy: Lasting Happiness in a Changing World* (New York: Avery, 2016).

18 See https://www.adec.org

19 Lizzy Miles, *Somewhere In Between: The Hokey Pokey, Chocolate Cake, and The Shared Death Experience* (Columbus: Trail Angel Press, 2011).

20 Raymond A. Moody, Jr., M.D., Ph.D. with Paul Perry, *Glimpses of Eternity: Sharing a Loved One's Passage from This Life to the Next* (Paradise Valley, AZ: SAKKARA Productions Publishing, 2010).

21 Eckl, *A Beautiful Death*, p. 167-169.

22 Maggie Callanan and Patricia Kelley, *Final Gifts: Understanding the Special Awareness, Needs, and Communications of the Dying* (New York: Simon & Schuster, 1992).

23 David Kessler, *Visions, Trips, and Crowded Rooms: Who and What You See Before You Die* (New York: Hay House, 2010).

24 For a synopsis and history of the musical, see https://en.wikipedia.org/wiki/Peter_and_the_Starcatcher, accessed 4-12-22.

25 Eckl, *A Beautiful Joy*. p. 101.

26 John O'Donohue, *Anam Cara: A Book of Celtic Wisdom* (New York: HarperCollins-Perennial, 1997).

27 Eckl, *Sparks of Celtic Mystery: soul poems from Éire* (Livingston, MT: Flying Crane Press, 2019) p. 85.

28 *Merriam-Webster's Collegiate Dictionary, 11th Edition* (Springfield, MA, 2004).

29 Eckl, *Poetics of Soul & Fire*, p. 19.

30 To learn more about Soul Poetics, see Eckl, *Reflections on Being Your True Self in Any Situation*, p. 76-85.

31 Eckl, *A Beautiful Joy*, p. 49-51.

Something in us knows—
joy comes at a cost
which many souls have dearly paid
as angel arrows pierced their hearts
with a living flame of Love that burned,
then quickly filled them up
with its unfathomable presence.

And in those moments
our hearts confirm that we are one
with Love's alchemical power
that transfigures us into itself.

WHY I WRITE

I write to understand my life, my mission,
my strengths and my vulnerabilities.

I write as a way for my Wise Inner Counselor
to explain to me more than I can comprehend
with my human intellect.

I write as a portal into the mind and heart
of my twin flame, Stephen.

When he was alive and easing toward his exit
from this world, we wrote poems and meditations
to express aspects of our love
that otherwise were too deep for words.

We still do.

For more information about Cheryl's books, videos and audios,
please visit www.CherylEckl.com.

CPSIA information can be obtained
at www.ICGtesting.com
Printed in the USA
JSHW032239260922
31028JS00006B/49

9 781734 645095